Rugs as an Investment

Rugs as an Investment
by Parviz Nemati

AGATE PRESS
New York
CHARLES E. TUTTLE COMPANY
Rutland, Vermont and Tokyo, Japan
1980

Printed in the United States of America by
LaSalle Industries, New York, New York
Leslie Schweiloch, Project Director

Paper: Warren 80 pound Lustro Offset Enamel Dull
Type: Sabon, set by Southern New England Typographic Service

Design: Leslie Ellis Smith
Drawings: John Batki
Photography: Thomas Feist, Ernest Silva

Library of Congress Catalogue Card Number: 79-53999
ISBN: 0-937266-01-9

In memory of

a great teacher and friend

Moni Pontremoli

ACKNOWLEDGEMENTS

For their rich inspiration in the field of Oriental art and weaving, I wish to thank Maurice Dimand and the late Richard Ettinghausen of the Metropolitan Museum of Art, and the staff of the Textile Museum of Washington, D. C. I am particularly grateful to my publishers, Jai Imbrey and Leslie Smith, who shared and sustained my enthusiasm in writing *Rugs as an Investment*. Jeanne Weeks, John Batki, Peggyann Chevalier, Tom Feist, Isolde McNicholl and Les Schweiloch deserve special thanks for their assistance and advice in the preparation of this book.

CONTENTS

Page 11   Foreword by the author

15   I   INVESTING IN RUGS

15   Tangible and Intangible Investments
18   History of Investing/Collecting
26   The Current Rug Market
34   Determining Value in Rugs
39   Active Market Trends
42   Short and Long Term Investing

54   II   A HISTORY OF RUG MAKING

54   Origins
55   History of Rugs up to the 19th Century

70   III   TECHNIQUES OF RUG MAKING

70   Materials
71   Dyes
75   Knotting and Weaving Techniques
79   Basic Elements of Design
                      Decorating with Oriental Rugs

91   IV   PERSIAN RUGS

95   Western and Northwestern Persian Rugs
99   Central Persian Rugs
102   Eastern and Southern Persian Rugs

107   V   TURKISH RUGS

111   Rugs from the Istanbul Area
114   Anatolian Rugs
115   Anatolian Village Rugs

119   VI   CAUCASIAN RUGS

126   Kazak Region Rugs
127   Karabagh Region Rugs
130   Talish Region Rugs
131   Kuba-Shirvan Region Rugs
135   Daghestan Region Rugs

139   VII   TURKOMAN RUGS

146   Salor Rugs
146   Saryk Rugs
146   Tekke Rugs
146   Yomud Rugs
147   Ersari Rugs
150   Balouch Rugs

CONTENTS

151	VIII	INDIAN RUGS
151		Moghul Rugs
154		19th and Early 20th Century Rugs
155	IX	CHINESE RUGS
155		East Turkestan Rugs
158		Early Chinese Rugs
159		Characteristics of 19th and 20th Century Rugs
162		Chinese Symbols
167	X	EUROPEAN RUGS
167		Spanish Rugs
167		French Rugs
170		English Rugs
174	XI	CURRENTLY AVAILABLE AND NEW RUGS
174		Available Old Rugs
178		New Iranian Rugs
179		New Pakistani Rugs
179		New Indian Rugs
179		New Afghanistani Rugs
182		New Turkish Rugs
183		New European Rugs
183		New Rugs from the Soviet Union
187		EXHIBITIONS AND MAJOR COLLECTIONS
190		BIBLIOGRAPHY
194		GLOSSARY/INDEX
203		LIST OF DEALERS

PLATES

Plate			Page		Plate			Page
	1	PASHMINA HERIZ	14			52	HEREKE SILK	112
	2	TABRIZ	16			53	OUSHAK	113
	3	HERIZ SILK	17			54	BERGAMA	116
	4	SERAPI	20			55	YORUK	117
	5	HADJI JALILI TABRIZ	21			56	KAZAK	120
	6	GHIORDES	24			57	SEWAN KAZAK	121
	7	CHINESE SILK	25			58	SILEH KAZAK	124
	8	ISFAHAN	28			59	KAZAK	125
	9	HEREKE	29			60	BORDJALOU KAZAK	128
	10	MASHAD	32			61	SHIRVAN	129
	11	HADJI JALILI TABRIZ	33			62	KHILA	132
	12	MOHTASHAM KASHAN	36			63	LENKORAN RUNNER	132
	13	MOHTASHAM KASHAN	37			64	SEICHUR	133
	14	SAROUK	40			65	TALISH	136
	15	SERAPI	41			66	KUBA KARABAGH	136
	16	SHIRVAN	44			67	MARASALI PRAYER	137
	17	KAZAK	45			68	HATCHLI PRAYER	140
	18	CHICHI	48			69	TEKKE	141
	19	SHIRVAN	49			70	YOMUD	144
	20	PEREPEDIL (KUBA)	52			71	BESHIR BOKHARA	145
	21	ERSARI	53			72	BELOUCH	148
	22	TABRIZ	56			73	BELOUCH	149
	23	NORTHWEST PERSIAN	57			74	ZIEGLER MAHAL	152
	24	KULA PRAYER	60			75	AGRA	153
	25	MELAS PRAYER	61			76	PEKING CHINESE	156
	26	MAMELUKE	64			77	CHINESE SILK	157
	27	SERAPI	65			78	CHINESE	160
	28	SHIRVAN	68			79	CHINESE RUNNER	161
	29	SHIRVAN	69			80	COLUMN RUG	161
	30	BIDJAR KILIM	72			81	YARKAND	164
	31	SENNEH KILIM	73			82	SEICHUR	165
	32	DHURRIE	76			83	SHUSHA KARABAGH	168
	33	SOUMAK	77			84	SAVONNERIE	169
	34	SOUMAK RUNNER	80			85	HEREKE SILK	172
	35	HAMADAN CAMELHAIR	80			86	QUM SILK	173
	36	AFSHAR	81			87	TABRIZ	176
	37	BAKHTIARI	84			88	KERMAN	177
	38	SAROUK	85			89	TEHRAN	180
	39	INTERIOR	88			90	BERGAMA	181
	40	INTERIOR	88			91	AFSHAR	184
	41	INTERIOR	89			92	FERAHAN	185
	42	SERAPI	92			93	DAGHESTAN PRAYER	188
	43	ANTIQUE SENNEH	93			94	KUBA	189
	44	FERAHAN (MALAYER)	96			95	SHIRVAN	192
	45	HERIZ	97			96	PEREPEDIL	193
	46	RAVAR KERMAN	100			97	SHIRVAN	196
	47	KASHAN	101			98	SEICHUR	197
	48	SAROUK	104			99	GENDJE KAZAK	200
	49	GHASHGAI	105			100	KUBA	201
	50	GHIORDES PRAYER	108			101	GHASHGAI SADDLEBAG	204
	51	SIVAS PRAYER	109			102	KERMAN SHAWL	205

There are certain sights and sounds that I remember vividly from my boyhood in the rug-weaving center of Kerman, in Iran. Dark, wet, freshly dyed wool drying on neighboring rooftops was as familiar a part of the landscape as the mountains encircling the arid plains of my region. I can still see the shady rooms with dirt floors where young girls—known as "bafande"—worked steadily, fingers flying as they tied the knots that became exquisite rugs. As they worked, these girls counted the knots in chanting voices, and I often woke to this rhythmic sound in the early morning, when the air was still cool and the light was fresh.

One incident in particular stands out in my memory. I was about thirteen, and my grandfather was holding a reception in our home for several foreign diplomats and government officials (above). Honoring his guests in the traditional way, he had spread rugs from the family workshop over our courtyard and out to the street. To me, nothing could have been more spectacular than this lush, colorful pavement, and yet my grandfather felt otherwise, for he muttered, "I hope they will stop producing these damn rugs."

After our guests had left, my grandfather explained to my brothers and me that he resented the people of "Farangistan" (the Western world) telling our weavers how to practice their art. Imagine: in placing orders for rugs, our guests had specified not only size, but color and design as well. To my grandfather, this was pure heresy, for he feared that it was only a short step from made-to-order rugs to mass production.

And he was right.

Prior to the early twentieth century, the designs woven into Oriental rugs, and the distinctive artistry of each rug-weaving area, reflected an uninterrupted cultural and historical tradition stretching back thousands of years. Like an exotic language, this remarkable legacy remained faithful to its origins, and at the same time allowed enormous range in the creation of the arabesque or geometric motifs and color harmonies that constitute each rug's unique appeal. The weavers who made these rugs were trained from early childhood in the grammar and vocabulary, so to speak, of their village or regional traditions; with mastery of the craft came the almost poetic ability to incorporate into the local designs personal variations expressive of deeply held individual spriritual beliefs.

But around the turn of the century, as the stream of orders from importers and European dealers began to grow, indigenous patterns were discarded or arbitrarily combined. The old natural dyes gave way to cheaper and inferior substitutes; the overall quality of weaving suffered under the pressure of rising demand and the need to speed up production.

So it was clear to me from an early age that although excellent rugs would not vanish overnight, they would become rare. Over the years, of course, this is exactly what has happened. And yet, while masterpieces of painting and sculpture have been labeled "works of art" and have achieved enormous value as investments (Rembrandt's *Aristotle Contemplating the Bust of Homer* sold for $2.3 million in 1961; Frederic Church's *Icebergs* fetched $2.5 million in 1979), the Oriental rug has remained a consistently undervalued and unappreciated art form. Unlike most masterpiece paintings and sculptures, high-quality rugs have not disappeared from the market: it is still possible to collect good, and even exceptional, pieces—though these are becoming increasingly scarce. To put it plainly, Oriental rugs represent an important and exciting new investment opportunity.

Before their exploration has progressed very far, the portfolio manager and the budding collector will find that astonishingly little has been published on the subject of Oriental rugs. To date, rug books have tended to fall into one of two categories: scholarly studies that focus on historically important pieces in museums or private collections, and sales catalogues that offer elaborate illustrations but very little informative text.

In writing this book, I have tried to combine information *and* illustration. Moreover, the rugs described are still available in today's market; they are mostly affordable, and (not to be overlooked) quite functional. Indeed, in

this field, form and function—or pleasure and use—can hardly be separated: these rugs were made to be useful as well as decorative—to be walked upon, sat upon, lived upon. And like most objects of true intrinsic quality, they improve with age: colors mature, fibers soften, some might even say that the rug's "soul," the gift of the weaver's hand and eye, mellows along with the more tangible aspects.

The book begins with an overview of investing because, as with any other commodity, it is important that investing in rugs be viewed as a science with rules of its own. A brief history of the early art of Oriental rugs sets the scene, followed by a discussion of the techniques of rug making. Then major rug-producing areas are brought up to date; the pieces described in detail are primarily nineteenth- and twentieth-century examples of rugs woven in Persia (Iran), Turkey, the Caucasus (Soviet Union), Turkestan, India, and China. Finally, a special chapter considers new investment-quality pieces.

My original intention was to illustrate many more examples of each type of rug. However, during the preparation of the book, I found that the limitation of space compelled me to select a much smaller number. I concluded along with my publishers that the only way of doing justice to the great wealth of rug types was to follow this edition directly with a series of books in which each volume will be devoted to a separate weaving area.

Throughout the text, the viewpoint is practical. How could it be otherwise? I grew up with rugs and have devoted my adult life to studying them, buying and selling them, touching them, and unavoidably, loving them.

Here, then, is an insider's view. In discussing the investment value of Oriental rugs, the availability of fine pieces, the international market, and the crucial role of the dealer in the acquisition and sale of rugs, I have taken a down-to-earth, commonsense approach. It is my hope that this book will encourage a wider public to know, to appreciate, and ultimately to collect the woven heritage of the East.

New York, 1980   Parviz Nemati

Plate 1
PASHMINA HERIZ 12′ x 9′
pashmina wool, c. 1780
An exceptionally rare early example
woven with a soft, lustrous wool usually used in the making
of the finest shawls for the nobility.

CHAPTER I

Traditionally veiled in mystique, Oriental rugs long remained one of the least understood forms of investment, but over the last few years, they have been recognized as one of the prime investments in the art and antiques market. In Europe and in the East, studies of investment trends indicate that rugs have been considered serious tangible investments for centuries, yet it is only recently that Americans have come to share this point of view.

By exploring the reasons for this rising interest, the investor in Oriental rugs will be prepared to select the investment plan to best suit his or her needs. In the last two decades, investment plans have been implemented for tangibles in the art and antiques field; rugs as investments, however, have their own particular history and properties. It is essential to first determine what rugs have in common with other forms of investments, and then what is unique to rugs themselves as tangible investments.

In both the antiques and financial markets, investment means the commitment of capital in order to augment its value over a period of time. Investing is a means of protecting capital against inflation, certain forms of taxation, and throwaway consumption. Investments may be divided into two general categories, tangibles (from the Latin *tangere*, "to touch") and intangibles. Both forms involve careful planning according to a set of guidelines: the allotment of capital, a time frame, and evaluation of risk. Intangible investments can be defined as the purchase of financial instruments, notes, bonds, equities, commodity futures, etc., for the purpose of earning interest, income, and often capital appreciation as well. With intangible investments, the investor's participation is for the most part limited to capitalizing the investment and reaping the benefits.

Tangible investments, on the other hand, may be defined as the acquisition of material assets with investment value—real estate, diamonds, gold, paintings, sculpture, and antiques—including Oriental rugs. Tangible investments are usually purchased primarily for use and pleasure, as in the case of furniture or paintings, and secondarily for resale value. Recently,

Plate 2
HADJI JALILI TABRIZ, 21′ x 14′
wool, late 19th Cent.
The great weaver's interpretation of the famous
"Ardebil Carpet" design.

however, important members of the financial community have begun to recognize the primarily financial gain potential of tangible investments. In 1979, Citibank established an art investment consultation service for clients with several million dollars to spend on a balanced portfolio of art and antiques, with investment as the prime focus.

HISTORY OF
INVESTING/
COLLECTING

The recent surge of interest in Oriental rugs as works of art with investment value is a relatively novel phenomenon in the United States. Europeans have, for many years, seen rugs, like silver and jewelry, as solid investment and as collateral. A brief summary of collecting and investing in rugs in Western Europe and North America will outline the growing appreciation of this form of investment.

European
Investors

In Europe, the fascination with Oriental rugs reaches back at least eight hundred years. The Spanish, followed by the English, the Italians, and the Russians, demonstrated an early interest in collecting rugs. We know from domestic scenes painted by artists such as Lorenzo Lotto and Jan Vermeer that rugs were prized as early as the sixteenth century by upper-middle-class Dutch and Italians. These collections, however, pale in comparison with the holdings of the rich and powerful aristocracy, the Imperial Russian collection, for example, or the three-hundred-year-old accumulation of the Hapsburgs of Austria. The Hapsburg collection was finally unveiled at the Vienna Exhibition of 1891, which is recorded for us in a monumental catalogue. Around this time, scholars and collectors began to build up collections for major public exhibitions and museums, and Wilhelm von Bode at the Berlin Museum published the first important work on Oriental rugs.

Side by side with the impressive museum collections and expositions, commercial collectors arose in Europe. Vincent Robinson of London was a pioneering investor in this special group, with a career marked by his association with public shows.

In 1888, Vincent Robinson and Company purchased two large rugs referred to as the "Ardebil Carpets." Originally, the Persian Shah Ismail's son, Shah Tahmasp, had presented these rugs to the Ardebil Mosque where his ancestors were buried. These medallion rugs were remarkable for their tranquil, abstract beauty (no men or animals could be depicted in a rug

Plate 3
HERIZ, 5′3″ x 4′
silk, early 19th Cent.
A fine early example from a center known for its silks.
(Property of a European Investment firm)

destined for a mosque), for their immense size (roughly thirty-five by eighteen feet—approximately thirty million knots), and for their inclusion of a cartouche bearing lines from the poet Hafiz and a weaver's signature:

I have no refuge in the world other than thy threshold.
There is no protection for my head other than this entry.
The Work of the Slave of Thy Kingdom, Maqsud Kashani
in the year 946 (A.D., 1539)

For more than three centuries, the two carpets lay on the floor of the mosque, trodden daily by the unshod feet of hundreds of worshipers. In the 1880s, the authorities of the mosque, finding themselves in need of a substantial sum of money, decided to sell some of their rugs to the firm of Ziegler Brothers, of Manchester, England, who in turn sold them to Vincent Robinson. For several years thereafter nothing was heard of the rugs. Then, in 1892, the public was invited to view a single rug, "the finest in the world" and "in a state of perfect preservation." The price asked for the rug at the time was the unheard-of sum of £2,500—too much for even a national museum. However, an appeal launched by Sir A. W. Franks and the designer William Morris was so successful that the Victoria and Albert Museum in London was able to acquire the rug the following year.

What the public did not know (although the director of the museum obviously did) was that Robinson had amalgamated the two Ardebil Carpets: the border of the more damaged piece was used to painstakingly restore the border of the other. For a time the multilated piece was concealed, but eventually it was sold to an American collector on condition that it would never be displayed in Europe. Now in the Los Angeles County Museum of Art, this piece has been described by a noted historian, the German scholar Kurt Erdmann, as a "true ruin, but when washed . . . brilliant in its depth of coloring and therefore almost superior to its big brother in the Victoria and Albert." If it were possible to estimate the value of the Victoria and Albert carpet today, the figure would run into millions.

As exhibitions in Europe spurred commercial collectors, a similar phenomenon took place in the United States. In a sense, the 1876 Centennial Exhibition in Philadelphia introduced Oriental rugs to America. The rugs

American
Collector/
Investors

Plate 4
SERAPI, 18′5″ x 11′7″
wool, early 20th Cent.
A classic, bold example in very large dimensions.

were an outstanding attraction and made a lasting impression on the minds of those who saw them. The superb quality of these rugs suggested to Americans the aura of Eastern mysticism. William Sloane, the founder of W. J. Sloane, bought the entire collection from the exhibition, and his store was the first major retailing channel for Oriental rugs in America. He was so successful in selling the collection that he dispatched his own buyers to the Orient to replenish his stock.

Other department stores, such as Wanamaker, Marshall Field, B. Altman, and private companies, including Kent Costikyan of New York, followed suit and ordered Oriental rugs designed to meet the tastes of their American customers. This early boom in collecting was reflected by extremely high pre-Depression prices for Oriental rugs. In the thirties, prices dropped, not only because of the Depression, but also because antique rugs flooded the market from such sources as Amtorg, an enterprise established by a cash-hungry new Soviet state to exchange old rugs for Western currency.

Wealthy individuals, such as the Morgans, Vanderbilts, Fricks, and Astors, began fervently to amass magnificent rugs. Their wealth permitted them to travel to such exhibitions as the Viennese Kunstgewerbe Museum Oriental Rug Show in 1891, and to one the following year in South Kensington, England. It also opened the doors to the well-furbished houses of European royalty and nobility.

One of the chief suppliers to the great collectors was Vitall Benguiat, known as "the pasha," who supplied rugs to the wealthiest Americans just as Joseph Duveen supplied paintings and sculpture. After establishing a family firm in London, Benguiat, a Syrian by birth, sailed for the United States in 1898. He had built up a considerable business by purchasing old rugs throughout Europe in exchange for new ones; self-taught, he relied on his infallible eye to select great works of art. His collaboration with the American Auctioneer's Association (AAA), the first and most prestigious American auction house of the time, facilitated his meteoric rise to fame. The first of his many successful auction sales brought $100,000. Yet it was rumored that he never sold his prize rugs at auction, but handled the sales privately with famous collectors, including Henry Marquand and Hagop Kervorkian. Like

Plate 5
HADJI JALILI TABRIZ, 11'9" x 8'8"
wool, early 20th Cent.
An unusual asymetric medallion with a delicate
herati pattern.

most art dealers, Benguiat was constantly cash poor as he immediately reinvested his gains in even more costly merchandise. Today his rugs appear in major museum collections: the Metropolitan Museum of Art in New York City, and the Textile Museum in Washington, D.C. for example.

These American tycoons built their own oceangoing freighters to send on expeditions to the Orient. They even influenced and enacted import laws; the Morgan Act of 1906—a law still in effect—was sponsored by J. P. Morgan, who wanted to import large quantities of antiques. According to the *New York Times* of April 29, 1937, this act established the antiques industry in this country by sanctioning the duty-free entry of art and antiques over one hundred years old. (J. P. Morgan himself specialized in fifteenth-, sixteenth-, and seventeenth-century Persian masterpieces.)

Charles Yerkes was another spearhead of the collector-investor movement. The sale of his collection in 1910 marked the first auction devoted entirely to rugs. Another discerning collector, Charles Deering, had one of the finest collections of fifteenth-, sixteenth-, and seventeenth-century Persian rugs, including a superb "Polonaise" carpet, which the Austrian court had probably imported from Persia. The diversity of his collection owes much to Stephan Berberyan, a noted dealer, who, in conjunction with W. G. Thompson, published a large, handbound book illustrating some of Deering's more spectacular treasures.

A collection similar in range to Deering's was gathered by Hagop Kervorkian, an archaeologist and the founder of the Kervorkian Foundation. Forty-one of the masterpieces from his collection were last seen as a group in 1966 at the Metropolitan Museum of Art prior to their dispersal to various museums and universities.

One of the most judicious of the more recent collectors was Joseph V. McMullan, whose rugs (later donated to museums) formed the subject of a Metropolitan Museum of Art show in 1970. Thomas Hoving, in his preface to the illustrated catalogue, wrote: "The show demonstrates how with energy and perspicacity one individual can manage to assemble an outstanding collection even at a time when collecting has become difficult. Mr. McMullan achieved this distinction by acquiring not only much admired classical

Recent
American
Collectors/
Investors

Plate 6
GHIORDES, 7'10" x 4'9"
wool, mid 18th Cent.
A rare "Double Prayer" design from the "Age of the Tulip".

23

乾清宮備用

examples made for court and urban centers of the sixteenth and seventeenth centuries, but also the not yet appreciated minor masterpieces of later centuries made by simple village or tribal weavers."

In recent years, the best example of collecting is the investment made by the industrialist Andrew Rollins Dole. When the Robert C. Eldred Company, began to sell off the Dole estate in 1970, I was able to purchase a piece from this published collection: a Tabriz mosque rug, measuring 31'6" by 18', for $4,000. Since it was then considered such an oversize rug, I parted with it two years later for $8,000. (Today, I would gladly pay $40,000 for a similar piece.) In the same sale, another Tabriz rug, 16'6" by 10', went for $22,000. In a 1977 sale at Sotheby Parke Bernet in New York, an almost identical silk Tabriz was sold for $200,000. However, this is by no means the record-breaking price fetched for an Oriental rug: the Boston Museum of Fine Arts paid $400,000 for a rare silk Persian hunting rug in 1966; while in Geneva, Switzerland, a similar rug brought $330,536 in April 1978.

CURRENT
ORIENTAL
RUG MARKET

According to the available evidence, rugs show all the signs of a solid investment: a steady rise in price accompanied by an increased demand and a diminishing supply. No wonder the publicity about tangibles as a growing source of investment interest has included rugs in a prominent place. Major periodicals have reported very strong gains in Oriental rugs. *Barron's* noted the trend in 1976 by recording that Oriental rug imports were up 21 percent since 1970. Two years later, in 1978, the *Wall Street Journal* confirmed that there were fewer fine examples of Persian rugs on the market and *Business Week* stated that Oriental rugs had increased 1000 percent over the previous ten years. The article in *Barron's* went on to observe that several investment syndicates were reported to have started buying rugs in the 1960s. One syndicate, operating in Europe, evaluated its holding in Oriental rugs at $9 million at the time of purchase; by 1976 the net worth of this holding was estimated to be over $200 million.

Patterns of
Investment
in the U.S.

Given their long-established value on the international market, the recent emergence of Oriental rugs on the American market remains to be explained. There are two main factors to consider: the first is the general growth of the U.S. art and antiques market in the 1960s and 1970s; the

Plate 7
CHINESE, 10' x 8'
silk and precious metal thread, late 19th Cent.
A rare example with an inscription of an Imperial palace.
(Private Collection, New York)

second is the particular development of the rug market in the United States and abroad since the Great Depression of 1929.

Although the concept of acquiring precious Oriental rugs with investment in mind was, as we have seen, quite well established in the United States, and more particularly in Europe, investment in tangibles was still very much secondary to other forms of investment. For many years, the stock market reigned supreme as a major source of profit. Easy acquisition and high liquidity of shares, along with regular dividends, enhanced this type of investment. The American stock market was particularly attractive after World War II, when the United States was the only major country with a combination of sizable capital investment funds, quality management, and intact productive labor forces. As a consequence, the United States had considerable control over the economic and political development of other parts of the world. Virtually every manufacturing company was expanding at such a rate that it required public financing, which contributed to a boom in the stock market.

However, conditions have changed. The stock market is no longer as certain as it once was, and more and more shareholders are considering alternative forms of investment and a more balanced portfolio, including tangibles—real estate, diamonds, art, and antique Oriental rugs. The uncertainty of the stock market has been accompanied by inflation in most of the industrial nations. In inflationary periods, rugs, along with other forms of tangibles, have shown increases in value. Common investors are seeking other alternatives to low-interest savings accounts and bonds which are directly linked to the value of the dollar. Tangibles of quality, whose virtues are embodied in themselves, are less subject to fluctuations in currency, although not altogether independent from these variations. With the increased demand for a tight supply of tangibles, prices go up. But even if prices dip for a period, tangibles of good quality undoubtedly recover and advance. In the meantime, especially if the tangible is an Oriental rug, the owner has the pleasurable dividend of enjoying the holding, and watching it mellow with age while it increases in value. Predictably enough, the most common type of investment in rugs is a purchase for use.

Rugs as A Tangible
Investment

Plate 8
ISFAHAN, 14′4″ x 10′9″
wool, c. 1935
An exceptionally fine masterpiece of modern craftsmanship
based on historic examples.

Tax Advantages

Because rugs are classified as items of personal use, their purchase, unlike other forms of investment, is not taxed as a business gain. If a rug is purchased by a corporation, it can be considered a business expense (office improvement); as office furniture (technically) a rug depreciates in value and can be deducted accordingly. Or, like any other form of art and antiques, a rug can be donated to a museum at an appraisal higher than its purchase value. Individuals, especially those in the 50-percent tax bracket, have found such donations to be an effective means of reducing taxes, as well as being good public relations.

International Commodity

Since rugs are an international commodity, they may be traded virtually anywhere in the world, independent of, and even benefiting from, the fluctuations in currency and marketplace of any one country. For example, the current low of the U.S. dollar has made it possible for those with Swiss francs or deutsche marks to purchase rugs inexpensively in the United States, with considerable discounts for cash sales. On the other hand, demand for so-called "old" rugs (approximately ten to fifty years old) is extremely high in Germany, where there is a shortage. This means that German dealers are seeking old rugs from the best and most inexpensive source, the United States, and are willing to pay more for them than Americans. To maximize on sales in any quantity, such as the liquidation of a corporate art and antiques portfolio comprising rugs, it is necessary either to have a keen feel for the market or to act through an agent experienced in international trade.

Growth in Prices

To show the gains in certain rug types, a Viennese dealer published a price index of the years 1955 to 1980 for several selected types of Oriental rugs. Using the year 1976 for the base figure of 100 for each rug type, by 1979 Heriz rose to 198, Sarouk to 224, Shiraz and Ghasghai registered even stronger gains at 250 and 256 respectively, Bokharas rose to 193, Kazak to 269, and Shirvan was the strongest at 295. These figures involve some flexibility, as no two handmade rugs are alike, and market trends vary from country to country and from year to year. These figures do, however, provide some indication of (a) the overall rapid rate of growth in rug prices, (b) the differential that makes certain rug types better investments than others at various times, and (c) the rise of an international rug market with a steady standardization of the cost of objects of quality. This means an increased liquidity of the investment merchandise.

Plate 9
HEREKE, 19'6" x 16'3"
wool, c. 1900
Commissioned by King Farouk of Egypt for his private
mosque in the Cairo palace.

But, in spite of recent growth in prices, Oriental rugs are still underpriced in comparison with virtually all other art forms. Pieces of antique French furniture, according to R. H. Rush, author of *Antiques as an Investment,* were worth 578 in 1965, compared to a base value of 100 in 1926. Antique rugs and carpets, even in 1980, have not caught up with pre-Depression prices. There are several reasons for this underpriced market. Until quite recently in the United States, rugs were not considered works of art or collectibles, but were thought of primarily as functional and decorative objects, and were dispensible whenever the owner decided to redecorate. The inroads of wall-to-wall carpeting may have decreased the demand for handwoven rugs. Now the cult of anything new—from cars to carpets—is fading in favor of the appeal of the old.

For a variety of reasons, the United States is an outstanding source of rugs and carpets for investment purposes. Many old and antique pieces came to this country along with refugees from Europe and Asia, a great many rugs were brought in because of the high international purchasing power of the dollar after the Second World War. More recently, the sixties and seventies saw the dispersal and sale of substantial collections of family heirlooms. Finally, in comparison to the foreign market until now, lack of local demand and the low dollar have encouraged European and Middle Eastern buying. All these factors make the United States a chief source of investments in antique rugs, but this is rapidly changing.

United States as Source of Antique Rugs

Many Americans are surprised that the United States is probably the best place to buy rugs. On one occasion, a client boasted to me of her prize possession, a small Daghestan prayer rug that she had purchased in Beirut. She produced a snapshot of the rug for my inspection. To her great surprise, I named the Lebanese dealer, gave the location of his shop, and pointed out an almost invisible repair in the corner of the rug. As it happened, a few years earlier I had sold the piece to a foreign dealer. My client's mortification increased when she learned the difference between what she paid for the piece in Beirut and what she could have paid in the United States.

Plate 10
MASHAD, 10'9" x 7'2"
wool with silk selvedge, c. 1935
Woven and signed by Amoghli, under commission by Reza Shah
Pahlavi for the Imperial palace.

VALUE OF RUGS

New Awareness

Determining Value
in Rugs

Authenticity

New scholarship in a field with comparatively little written documentation has accomplished two major tasks: first, it has increased the public's awareness of Oriental rugs as an art form with a rich history of its own, comparable to paintings and sculpture. (Recent museum exhibitions have also helped to expand public consciousness.) Second, this new information has allowed rugs to be more carefully identified and evaluated on the basis of date, provenance, and quality. And with the birth of publications such as *Hali* and *Rug News*, exclusively devoted to Oriental rugs, the gap in documentation is being slowly filled. Consequently, Oriental rugs are rapidly catching up in price with other works of art.

In the art and antiques market in which rugs are included, there are certain artistic and historic criteria that determine value, whether or not investment is the first consideration. Authenticity, rarity, quality, and condition set the intrinsic value of any work of art; utility, taste, fashion, and economic conditions affect the extrinsic value. These criteria by which all art forms are judged have specific applications in the evaluation of Oriental rugs.

Among the various factors, first and foremost is authenticity. Throughout the rug-producing world, each period evolved distinctive styles and types of rugs, integrating designs, colors, and materials which are difficult or nearly impossible to reproduce today. In great masterpieces, such as the Ardebil Carpet, it is not only the splendor of the weaving that gives the rug its value, but also the historic significance of the rug as one of the major representations of sixteenth-century northwest Persian art. The work itself is inimitable, given the inferior state of today's craftsmanship and materials, as well as the prevailing social and economic conditions. Such works also possess an abstract value as examples of the culmination of one of the richest periods in Islamic creativity, fusing art, literature, and outstanding quality.

Just as modern imitations of Jean-Baptiste Corot's paintings may have some decorative value, but next to the originals lack their brilliant tonalities and formal structure, early twentieth-century reproductions of a Ghiordes prayer rug will pale beside the authentic eighteenth-century pieces. At the same time, Oriental rugs, like many other art forms, accommodate their own share of translations and homages which are authentic on their own terms without

Plate 11
HADJI JALILI TABRIZ, 18'9" x 12'7"
wool, late 19th Cent.
The design is a variation of the "Ardebil" type.

pretension to originality. These interpretations can have definite value for lovely color effects or superb workmanship, as in the new Tabriz based on an Ardebil design (see plate 2). But, in the same way that Twentieth-century fakes of Jan Vermeer paintings have been passed off as originals, certain modern rugs have been sold as antiques. More commonly in the rug field, genuine antique pieces with heavy repair or alteration have been shown as works in mint condition (for example, the Ardebil Carpet at the Victoria and Albert Museum).

Rarity is another determinant of value. The surviving paintings of Leonardo da Vinci are so rare that were we to encounter one on the market, its value would be incalculable. Similarly, the oldest surviving knotted rug, from the fifth century B.C. funeral mounds at Pazyryk, has a priceless value, a thus far unassailable uniqueness. Other rugs fall into types whose relative rarity is determinable: roughly a few hundred Safavid pieces survive; there may be approximately one thousand "Transylvania type" prayer rugs. Within any one category, other scales of value must be considered. For example, the relative scarcity of white-ground antique rugs—such as the remarkable eighteenth century Heriz featured on the cover—carries a special premium.

Certain rugs are rare by virtue of their esoteric nature. The Mohtasham Kashan is unique in its representation of an episode from the *Shah-nameh (A King's Book of Kings)*: the hero Rustam surrounded by tamed div (demons) and subdued wild animals (plate 13). A single page of this manuscript of Persian miniatures sold for $573,000 at Sotheby's in London in 1978. It is therefore not surprising that this specially commissioned rug of the same subject should command a tag of $75,000. On the other hand, the so-called great representative of a type is also enthusiastically sought by some collectors. For example, the highly characteristic Serapi represents the acme of weaving for this type (plate 4).

Age adds value to a rug, in general, but counts for more or less according to provenance. Most older Turkoman rugs date from the nineteenth century; the very few verifiably eighteenth-century pieces, such as the Ersari Beshire (plate 21), command a high price, mostly because of the great rarity of their age. However, relative age differences within the nineteenth-century Turkoman

Rarity

Age

Plate 12
MOHTASHAM KASHAN, 6′9″ x 4′5″
wool, mid 19th Cent.
Pictured are Nadir Shah, conqueror of India, and his Court.

37

group may not make that much difference, whereas tribal attribution would. Also, age is not an absolute criterion: what may be old for a Sarouk could be recent for a Heriz.

Condition

Material condition plays a definite role in assigning value. If there are two very similar pieces, the one in finer condition carries the higher price tag. But this rarely occurs; we have rugs in good condition, and pieces in damaged, restored, patched, incomplete, even fragmentary states. Very old specimens are usually worn, so the factor of material condition may not be that much of a deterrent to the potential collector-buyer. (Of course, worn condition may not always be a sign of age: some new rugs may wear faster than old ones.) Therefore, condition is most important in setting value for relatively new, easily available rugs that are purchased for decorative, or short-term investment value. The decorative aspect of rugs varies with the swing of fashion, and is yet another factor in determining value.

Quality

Yet the ultimate determinant of value, in the case of long-term investment in rugs, is the quality of the piece, both aesthetic and technical. Quality is that elusive, variously sensible, and nearly inexpressible *something* in an object that makes us want to look, touch, *feel* it again—or, to turn away in disgust. As for technical determinants, most experts will agree on these after some inspection of the object under discussion. We ascertain the materials: fine wool, or soft silk; we delight in the glow of unadulterated natural colors; we appreciate the delicacy of knotting, the elegance of end and side finish. When we come to artistic quality, the arena opens up and fierce aesthetic battles may ensue between proponents of different views. Some will prefer the sea-green, others the brick-red Eagle Kazaks. The connoisseur of sophisticated Samarkand rugs in silk, gold, and silver will look down on the collector of boldly "primitive" Caucasian rugs. In fact, the understanding of artistic creation in rugs depends on no absolute criteria, but it is a combination of the merits of the piece—its boldness, originality, harmony of conception and execution—and the viewer's sensitivity and knowledge to see the excellence. How often will a collector bemoan the premature release of an early acquisition, saying "If only I knew back then!" It requires patient study, often years, to appreciate the value of what has taken decades of experience and deep inspiration to produce.

Plate 13
MOHTASHAM KASHAN, 6'9" x 4'5"
wool, mid 19th Cent.
Depicted here are King Solomon (top) and Rustam, hero
of The King's Book of Kings (Shah-Nameh).

Once we understand the multiplicity of criteria that go into assigning a value to a specific rug, it becomes easier to see why in fact this value has survived through the ages and across continents, as all artistic value has always survived. Under the guise of usefulness, rugs crept underfoot in nearly every culture and asserted themselves on artistic grounds. And lasting value goes with lasting demand.

Recently, certain markets for Oriental rugs have been extremely active, most notably tribal rugs. The rapid depletion of resources in this sector partially explains this. The disappearance of the tribes, causing the disintegration of the sources for woven tribal art, has caused a tremendous demand among collectors, especially in Europe. As foreshadowed by the high prices, the finer pieces may vanish from the market over the next ten years. Small tribal rugs and bags are reaching up to $25,000, as did a Turkoman Osmolduk (bagface) at a Paris auction in 1979. In these categories, it would appear that investors are trying to corner the market with some success. **ACTIVE MARKET TRENDS**

Equally popular for use and investment have been the antique traditional rugs from Persia, Turkey, the Caucasus, and China, e.g., Kashans, Isfahans, Herekes, and Pekings. There is keen competition for these last from the general public to the noted collectors. As the best examples are already in museum collections, very few appear on the market. Savonnerie and other famous marks from Europe may improve, after experiencing a slight fall-off after the 1950s; they have been slowly picking up in the last few years and therefore have excellent potential.

The new rugs, made within the last twenty years, have been rapidly acquired by U.S. and Near Eastern buyers, mostly for domestic use and not as investments.

The decorator market has its own special angles. There has been a general rise in interest over the last fifteen years in Oushaks, Heriz, Serapis, Tabriz, dhurries, and kilims, mainly for decorative purposes, with investment value either of no concern or as a secondary purpose. Trends in decorative fashion must be followed by an astute investor.

Investing wisely involves a careful consideration of every aspect of the field, as well as the buyer's own needs. These needs may be decorative, with investment in mind, or purely investment-oriented. **ASSESSING INVESTOR'S NEEDS**

Plate 14
SAROUK, 12'2" x 9'2"
wool, early 20th Cent.
A fine early Sarouk from the Mahajeran workshop.

40

To choose a rug as a decorative piece with practical use in mind, one must first decide the amount to be allocated to the purchase, keeping realistic market prices in view. It is wise to allow for some flexibility. A second and equally important consideration is that of size. Here again, some flexibility is advisable, since few handmade carpets of age come made to size, and altering a fine rug greatly affects not only the beauty and effect of the design, but also the resale value. A case in point is a fine antique Serapi which was cut down to accommodate a living room in upstate New York; it is now assessed at 70 percent of its value when intact. Alternate solutions to the problem of wrong size should be entertained, two rugs in place of one, perhaps. Another consideration in choosing a rug is quality. With the tremendous variety of designs and weaves of rugs, it is advisable to familiarize yourself with the various types available on the market by reading handbooks, visiting dealers, and touring museums. This will make you, the potential purchaser, aware of the great range of quality within any given type of rug.

Specific needs should be carefully weighed. Will the rug be subject to a great deal of traffic, such as in an entrance hall, or a dining room where chairs constantly slide? If so, you must add to your list of requirements a strong weave. For strength of weave, Bidjars may be recommended, while silks, particularly antique pieces, should be hung or kept in areas without traffic. If the rug will be exposed to strong sunlight, you might have to restrict your choice to certain types of colors. However, if you purchase a relatively new rug with strong colors, you may in fact wish to have the strident tones mellowed by gentle fading in the sunlight, which will add a valued patina to your rug.

Short-Term
Investment

If decorative purpose is only secondary to investment value, you must decide whether the investment is short term or long term (three years or more). If the client is interested in short-term investment, I would advise the purchase of commercial, fast-selling rugs. This kind of investment will naturally be subject to the swings of fashion and the situation of the market. It helps to be aware of current trends in interior design, and the types, sizes, and color schemes in favor. This kind of investment is extremely difficult because the market is volatile, and it must be done in conjunction with dealers who are portfolio-manager advisors and who keep in close touch with the market. It is comparable to trad-

Plate 15
SERAPI, 14′1″ x 12′4″
wool, late 19th Cent.
This piece contains a border with poems by the
14th Century poet, Hafez.

ing in stock options as opposed to purchasing stock outright. If handled correctly, these manipulations may be extremely lucrative. But since this is a high-risk investment, portfolio managers usally prefer the long-term investment pieces.

When the client is interested in long-term investment, I believe in carefully researching the market for currently underpriced rug types. The reasons for the underpricing may be various: absence of documentation and consequently poor exposure are usually key reasons for the availability of a certain type. After researching the market, I will often discover that upcoming publications, museum shows, or auctions may drive up the price of a given rug type in a certain period of time. Other factors that play a role in rising prices are the exhaustion of a given type of rug or the changing political situation in the producing country. Then, in accordance with the set capital, I discreetly begin to assemble a collection of a particular type of rug. Without the utmost discretion, other speculating dealers could artificially boost the market I am seeking to take over. Long-Term Investment

These are only the outlines of a strategy to build any significant collection with long-term investment value. Once the collection is established, the task of upgrading it will take more effort. This means acquiring rarer pieces of the type collected, or replacing one example with a similar but superior piece.

In place of the hypothetical beginner investor, let us look at some actual kinds of investors. The first, or common, investor is the buyer interested in acquiring rugs for use. Far different are the aims of the *collector,* who is usually looking for a specific type of rug within a given area, such as Chichi rugs (a particular type of Kuba, plate 18), or a special format, perhaps prayer rugs. His or her sole concern will be finding examples that reflect the cultural, technical, and historial aspects of the chosen type or types of rugs. COLLECTOR-INVESTORS

In most cases, the collector does not initially assemble a collection as an investment. Yet some of the best investments have resulted from this approach. It is probably because the collector exercises great care in searching for the best examples of a given type. In collecting, the aesthetic and historical value outweighs the condition and price of the piece. Very often, initial purchases are inexpensive but special examples, usually in need of extensive repairs. Over the The Collector

Plate 16
SHIRVAN, 9'5" x 5'7"
wool, early 20th Cent.
A collector's rug from a district known for its fine
weave and excellent designs.
(Private Collection, New York)

years, the collector becomes familiar with the names and history of a given weaving area and begins to concentrate on a certain period and locality. The collector then begins to upgrade the collection, becoming more and more selective. In most cases, the collector befriends a dealer who is knowledgeable in the same area. By using the expertise of the dealer and constantly exchanging inferior pieces for better examples, the collector successfully assembles an important collection. As the quality is upgraded, the investment value is significantly increased.

The "Rug Freak"

Occasionally a collector will jokingly refer to himself as a rug freak, or "ruggie," or even "rug-bug." After a few initial transactions at a low budget, this type of collector is inevitably hooked, especially after one or two intriguing and profitable turnovers. And—the rug-bug changes from a collector into a collector-investor. Typically this person is highly educated, possibly an academic. Before long, an originally skeptical spouse, who used to complain about this passion for "old rags," will be selling the household valuables, from pianos to diamonds, to support a habit that is no longer just fun, but profitable as well. Fairly soon, the collector may be leaving the academic life to become a full-fledged dealer-collector of Oriental rugs.

The Investment-Minded Collector

The investment-minded collector differs from the self-styled rug freak at the outset. From the very beginning he buys only important and costly rugs, usually in perfect or near-perfect condition. There is a long tradition of this form of collecting in Germany and Switzerland, as well as in other European countries. A good example of an investment-minded collector is a Swiss physician who came to me for the first time in the mid-sixties. After two days of rummaging through my entire inventory, he selected just one rug. But what a rug it was. It happened to be the most expensive piece in my whole stock. Since then, after fifteen years of buying exclusively from me, he has retained the same fastidiousness he demonstrated on his first visit. I have to admire his combination of artistic eye and shrewd business sense. When we recently discussed the value of his collection, I jokingly offered double what he originally paid for the first piece. He replied, with a grin, that I would be lucky if he chose to sell it at ten times the cost. Alas, he was right.

Plate 17
KAZAK, 7'3" x 5'2"
wool, 19th Cent.
An unusual "Eagle" design in perfect condition.

The dealer-investor is that extremely knowledgeable person who has more time to devote to locating particular rugs than did our Swiss collector-investor. Through connections and expertise, the dealer-investor devotes himself almost exclusively to buying and selling select rugs. The dealer-investor distinguishes himself from the ordinary dealer by his special attention to a particular sector of the market, and by his flexibility in deciding whether to buy or sell. Whereas the average dealer runs a high turnover business, constantly buying and selling inventory, the dealer-investor follows the investment trends and buys and sells accordingly. Whereas the dealer marks up all items at a set percentage, the dealer-investor plays the market. He may, for example, choose to dispose of a certain kind of stock if he finds the market for that type on the downslide—or, conversely, he may hold on to certain inventory if he foresees that type becoming fashionable or rare in the future.

The Dealer-Investor

Many portfolio managers and trust departments of banks and mutual funds, particularly in Europe, have recently stepped up their holdings in tangibles, including Oriental rugs. These managers usually begin by establishing rapport with one expert, and subsequently buy exclusively through this dealer. In such high-finance deals, the manager must obtain the complete discretion of the dealer who supplies him. When the portfolio manager needs to purchase a large group of rugs for a given portfolio, he has to work with a special kind of dealer capable of advising him, and of being instrumental in acquiring the rugs. We shall call this dealer the consultant-dealer. Like the dealer-investor, he is thoroughly familiar with the market. What makes him special is his familiarity with long- and short-term investment plans, and his ability to act as an agent through his personal connections and his expertise in dealing with the needs of a large financial group. He has special insight into money and investment markets, as well as expert knowledge of the woven art form. He is able to complete an accurate catalogue of rug investments with specific attributions of provenance, rug type, quality, history, and condition. More specifically, the consultant-dealer has a broad knowledge of the international market in Oriental rugs and a keen grasp of past and present trends. A long-established network of dealers working in close association with him allows the consultant-dealer to be able to obtain a sufficient quantity of the sought merchandise, without inflating current prices. Toward this end, discretion is imperative to

The Consultant-Dealer

Plate 18
CHI CHI, 5'7" x 3'9"
wool, 19th Cent.
Chi Chi rugs are much sought after by collectors for
their rarity and design.
(Formerly from the Reed Collection)

48

assure complete privacy for the investor and his aims, with the object of securing extensive or exclusive holdings of a particular type of rug from a specific period (for example, buying all available nineteenth-century Eagle Kazaks).

Corporate Leasing Plans

An interesting option for corporate investors is the corporate leasing plan provided by some consultant-dealers. Several companies, who have recently taken on a greater number of international accounts, have used Oriental rugs to give their corporate headquarters a continental aura of elegance and sophistication. The leasing program offers them certain practical advantages of both an aesthetic and financial order. If a given company does not have sufficient capital at any one time to invest in a rug of sufficient quality for a corporate image-improvement program, the consultant-dealer will arrange to lease several outstanding rugs over a period of time, with the option to buy. The tax advantages of this type of leasing are similar to company-car leasing programs: payments are deductible as a business expense; and interest on the payments is totally deductible. The leasing agreement usually provides several useful services, including design consultation (independently, or with the corporation's interior-design staff), insurance coverage, restoration, repair, and periodic cleaning. In some cases, there is a provision for purchase over a certain time. Although this may cost the buyer more than an initial payment on a one-time basis, the overall cost will be compensated by the rise in the market price of the rugs.

The Co-Investor

Finally, a word about the co-investor. In the rug business, where capital gain is immediately reinvested into the business by acquiring more inventory, there is often a restricted cash flow. Yet cash is essential to constantly renew and enrich inventory before prices rise even higher, and most rug dealers are eager to have a ready supply of cash. However, the longer it takes to liquidate merchandise, the more the value of the inventory goes up (in a market of accelerated growth). It is therefore profitable to hold on to some merchandise for as long as possible. This is where the co-investor is a particularly valued partner for the rug dealer, and the co-investor may stand to make an excellent return.

In the early 1970s, I was approached by investors in tangibles whose main goal was to profit from the spiraling prices of rugs. This kind of investor did not want to assume the responsibility of actually selecting, holding, and liquidating

Plate 19
SHIRVAN, 5'6" x 3'7"
wool, late 19th Cent.
A typical example with a rare golden-yellow leaf
and chalice border.

the rugs. In the case of one client, a busy attorney, we proceeded as follows: we selected a rug which we knew to be readily salable within a given period of time. We sold the rug to the lawyer at 25 percent less than our retail price. We then immediately took the rug on consignment from him and sold it within six months for 5 percent above the original retail price. In this way, the co-investor avoided the time-consuming process of selection, maintenance, insurance, restoration, and perhaps warehousing. The co-investor then reinvested his original amount, and placed the profit toward building up his own personal collection.

In closing, a little advice on how and where to buy rugs. Remember, very few antique pieces are left on the market, and it is unlikely that these will be offered by the itinerant salespeople who occasionally hold auctions. Unless in an important estate sale, such as the von Hirsch sale in June, 1978, exceptional rugs do not appear at auction. The popularity of well-publicized sales precludes great bargains; by and large, poor to mediocre merchandise comes up for sale. At established auction houses, most of the pieces are often on consignment from dealers who find this an easy and quick means to dispose of stock. A dealer with an important rug generally prefers to advertise the piece as his own in order to establish his reputation as a dealer of quality, rather than anonymously offer it at auction. For the amateur rug collector, it is often difficult to examine pieces for hidden damage and repairs at auction viewings, where poor light, crowding, and regulations against touching do not permit close study. In addition, pieces are frequently miscatalogued because the auction experts lack time or training. Whenever good pieces do appear at auction, inexperienced buyers are usually outbid by dealers or appointed agents.

However, keeping a watch on the auction scene does help to establish an idea of market trends and availability of certain rug types. In the long run, it is most useful to have an agent, who has greater expertise in auction politics and more time to research the market—hence, the benefit of working with a dealer whom you can trust. For this purpose, a list of reliable dealers has been provided at the back of this volume.

BUYING;
AUCTION &
DEALERS

Plate 20
PEREPEDIL (KUBA), 6'7" x 4'6"
wool, c. 1930
A traditional design with a "Kufic" border.

A HISTORY OF
RUG MAKING

The art of the knotted rug reaches back into prehistory, but the majority of pieces at dealers, auctions, antique shops and shows, department stores, and even museum exhibitions are mostly products of the nineteenth and twentieth centuries. The authentic village and nomadic rugs, often crafted on small looms for local use, from Iran, Turkey, the Caucasus, East Turkestan, China, India, and Pakistan, and from Central Asia represent only a fraction of the rugs produced. Most of the known and collected examples reflect the weaving of workshops catering to the Western trade. After the second half of the nineteenth century, new materials and dye processes were introduced into rug making in an attempt to speed up production to meet the demands of the Western market. And in the 1880s, factories altered designs, colors, and textures of rugs. Yet many aspects of weaving remain surprisingly unchanged and, although the methods of production have become better organized and quite standardized, rugs continue to be made in many of the traditional places. This chapter will give a general overview of the early history of rug making; later chapters will deal specifically with the major rug-producing areas of the nineteenth and twentieth centuries.

ORIGINS OF
AN ANCIENT
TRADITION

The patterns and basic techniques are almost exclusively based on a formidable number of traditional formats coming down from antiquity. The exact origins of rug weaving cannot be traced. Kurt Erdmann places the origin in East Turkestan, where sheep-herding nomads made these easily transported rugs for floor coverings and bedding in their tents, to protect them from the cold. Unfortunately, we know very little about the earliest examples of knotted rugs. A relatively small number of them, which we will discuss, have been preserved in great museums and private collections the world over (see list of museums, page 187), but the sad fact remains that, because of the perishable nature of the materials and through continuous use, the vast majority of older rugs are now gone.

Pazyryk
Carpet

We owe recovery of the earliest surviving knotted rug to the preservative quality of the Siberian ice in the Altai Mountains near the Outer Mongolian

Plate 21
ERSARI, 15'10" x 6'8"
wool, late 18th Cent.
A rare early example in exceptional condition
with a unique design.

border. The team of the Soviet archaeologist S. I. Rudenko discovered this piece, known as the Pazyryk Carpet, in a Scythian burial mound at Pazyryk in 1949. Even after a sleep of twenty-two centuries (according to carbon-14 test dating), the brilliant red and green tonalities continue to glow. The Pazyryk Carpet, measuring roughly six by six feet, with a dominant tile-work central motif surrounded by borders featuring rows of elks and carefully wrought horsemen, demonstrates a sophisticated artistic tradition. In 1978, the Turkish scholar, Nejat Diyarbekirli, convincingly argued that the Pazyryk rug is of Turkic origin because of the use of motifs related to Turkic artifacts and metalwork. Whether of Turkic manufacture or imported from some other more artistically advanced culture, the Pazyryk Carpet evinces a tradition of knotted textiles deeply rooted in antiquity.

As early as the eighth century B.C., sources from Egypt, Greece, Phoenicia, Mesopotamia, and Persia tell us that wealthy families frequently adorned their palaces with magnificent rugs, and that the production of rugs was based on a highly sophisticated industry. The *Book of Kings* recounts how the floors of the palace of Harun al Rachid displayed some 22,000 rugs woven in Khorassan. Perhaps the most valuable Persian ever woven was the "Spring of Khosrau" from the sixth century. The colossal rug (purported to measure about 11,300 square feet) was woven in silk, embroidered with gold and silver, and encrusted with jewels. It inspired the homage of poets and enlivened the palace of Khosrau I at Ctesiphon, but it was eventually hacked to pieces by the soldiers of the Mohammedan army.

The great period of creativity in the art of the rug took place in Persia during the Safavid times (1499–1722). During this period, all the resources and patronage of a resplendent court went into the expansion of a hitherto mostly nomadic craft. Primarily under the reigns of Shah Tahmasp (1524–1576) and Shah Abbas (1588–1629), Persian weaving became an established large-scale artistic and commercial enterprise revolving around major weaving centers. The rich artistic climate, where master miniaturists, calligraphers, philosophers, and mathematicians worked in harmony, with regular salaries and special commissions, gave birth to important schools of weavers. Court painters designed complex curvilinear floral patterns.

Plate 22
TABRIZ, 11′10″ x 8′4″
Cork wool with silk foundation, c. 1960
An opulent modern masterpiece recreating an authentic
17th Cent. Isfahan carpet, using historic methods.
Signed Amir Chatri.

Weavers were grouped under extremely rigid supervision to ensure the highest weaving techniques, using the finest wool and silk available, and colors that have remained unsurpassed to this day.

From this period came the most magnificent rugs of historic significance. Tabriz, Kashan, Herat, and perhaps Kerman, evolved into busy centers of production. The royal looms of Shah Abbas at Isfahan also worked for the early export trade. Large garden and vase carpets, often with inscriptions in cartouches, and elegant prayer rugs were among their prestigious and coveted output. The intensity of these finely knotted rugs rivaled that of the allied art forms of book illumination and calligraphy, a tradition that flourished into the eighteenth century. A northwest Persia carpet, with its overall floral pattern and lobed central medallion, clearly derives from the early court styles and exemplifies the creative genius of the age (plate 23).

The long reign of the Persian monarchy, while permitting a continuity in weaving during the eighteenth century, gradually became more self-absorbed, and royal patronage became a secondary factor in controlling the quality and quantity of rugs produced. Thus, the inspiration for such masterpieces as the Ardebil Carpets was eventually lost. Alongside the metropolitan tradition, a semi-nomadic output with roots buried deep in history began to surface in Western trade in the eighteenth century. The Kurds, Afshars, and Ghasghai wove forceful designs, often having little in common with the sophisticated city rugs (plate 49). The tribal rugs shared more, stylistically, with the weaving of the Caucasus.

Early
Ottoman
Weaving

Paralleling the great Persian tradition, the art of weaving also flourished in Turkey. The earliest surviving examples of Anatolian weaving follow the accounts of Khosrau's rug by six hundred years. Fragments from the thirteenth century, carefully kept in the great mosque of Ala-ad-Din in Konya (Turkey), reveal a mature Seljuk tradition of weaving with geometric patterns. (It was this weaving that Marco Polo praised as the 'finest in the world'.) The great wealth of symbols and rug types reflects the central position of Turkey as a crossroads of civilization. The mountainous plateau known as Asia Minor was occupied by successive waves of conquerors, from the

Plate 23
NORTHWEST PERSIAN, 12'4" x 7'6"
wool, c. 1800
Woven in the Karabagh district, then part of the
Persian Empire, this piece contains both Caucasian
and Persian motifs.

Hittites, Scythians, Greeks, Romans, Medes, Byzantines, Seljuk Turks, the Crusaders, Mongols, and, eventually, the Osmali or Ottoman Turks.

At about the same time as the Safavids, the competing Ottoman court developed its own line of high weaving art, having enriched itself with the carpet traditions of the Mamelukes of Egypt and Syria, two provinces conquered in the early sixteenth century. The Ottoman royal workshops began to produce rugs influenced by the Mameluke tradition of Cairo: geometric mosaic patterns with stars, octagons, squares, and triangles in cherry red, yellow-green, and pale blue. The seizure of Tabriz in 1514 brought an influx of master weavers from the Safavid court. By the late sixteenth century, the sultan's workshops had evolved a unique style, blending Cairene and Persian influence, which remained popular into the twentieth century.(plate 26)

By the seventeenth century, Western Anatolia had established heavy trade with Europe through its centers of Oushak, Bursa, and Bergama. Ghiordes, Ladik, Melas, and Konya specialized in prayer rugs. The splendor of the Turkish court style, exemplified by the prayer-rug format, reached its apogee in the eighteenth century.

The great intimacy of the Ottomans with the French kings led to an artistic exchange between the two nations. The French Savonnerie incorporated Turkish bird and flower designs, while the Turkish weavers adapted French floral and coat d'armes motifs. It is also from this time that the Turkish soldiers brought back the prized tulip bulbs to raise in the royal gardens of Seraglio. The favored royal flower was immortalized in the "Chintamani" design and widely symbolized the peace and prosperity of the age. The French influence was most pronounced under the Sultan Abdul Mejid, a Francophile known as "Monsieur Osman." At his newly established looms in Hereke, he initiated the "Mejid" Ghiordes style famed for its pink rose designs on a rich pistachio background (see p. 111).

The rise of the Mogul dynasty in India in the early sixteenth century produced a brief flowering of rug art. Babur, the Mongol conquerer of India and the founder of the Mogul dynasty, transformed the small industry of coarsely woven rugs into a magnificent art form, equaling the knotted

Early
Indian
Weaving

Plate 24
KULA PRAYER, 5'9" x 4'2"
wool, late 18th Cent.
An early example inscribed on the Lamp,"Ala-ad-Din" after
the mosque in Konya.

masterpieces of Safavid Persia. Spurred by the flaming rivalry between India and Persia, Akbar the Great (1556–1605) installed major court looms in northwestern India and imported master weavers from Persia. The Moguls set up large workshops at Agra, Lahore, and Fatpur with a fully salaried staff where artists from all areas of the arts received homage. Unfortunately, the height of Indian rug weaving was of a relatively brief duration, leaving few rugs from this period accessible today.

Early Chinese Weaving

In neighboring China, the flowering of rug making came a century later. The earliest Chinese official records referring to rug weaving date from the reign of the great patron of the arts, Emperor H'ang Hsi (1662–1722). This emperor invited Chinese painters in Peking to make rug designs, and he also sent abroad for foreign master-weavers. The height of rug weaving came during his grandson Ch'ien Lung's reign (1736–1796). At this time, rug making was established in workshops in Kansu, Shantung, and Peking. These workshops remained productive into the twentieth century. With Peking as a prominent center, Chinese rugs continued to be made with thick pile and simple color variations, embodying a rich language of symbols. Nonetheless, aside from the royal looms, most early Chinese rugs were produced in the northern and western provinces adjoining Mongolia, East Turkestan, and Tibet. Designs from this period continued to influence production into the late nineteenth and early twentieth centuries.

Early Tribal Weaving

Paralleling the proliferation of royal looms and urban weaving centers, nomadic and village weavers continued their centuries-old craft of knotted rugs, with the earliest surviving examples dating from the eighteenth century. In Persia, the village rugs reflected court tastes. In Turkey and the Caucasus, bold angular designs predominate. (Bergamas from Turkey and Kazaks from the Caucasus often have a very similar layout of geometric medallions and strong reds, blues, and greens.) In the Turkoman region of Central Asia, weavers continued to use their ancient tribal patterns of octagonal guls arranged in a grid.

The Turkomans

The first written records of the Turkomans appear in the work of ninth-century Arab historians, who referred to them as the Oghuz. Over the centuries, the Turkomans migrated from their eastern homeland near the

Plate 25
MELAS PRAYER, 3'9" x 3'8"
wool, c. 1800
A unique early example from an ancient Turkish weaving center.

Altai Mountains in Siberia until they occupied parts of today's northeastern Iran, northern Afghanistan and Pakistan, the Turkoman and Uzbek Soviet Republics, and Sinkiang in western China. The Turkomans are related to the earliest Seljuk and Ottoman settlers of Anatolia. A precise record of their migrations does not exist, since the Turkomans had no written tradition prior to the twentieth century. However, the records of Western travelers such as Arminius Vambery helped to locate the tribes in the last hundred years of their history.

A little more is known of the early history of another semi-nomadic group of weavers, the Caucasians. As early as the seventh century B.C., the traveling historian Herodotus noted the teeming diversity of the peoples of the Caucasus, and their skill in dyeing and weaving wool. By the tenth century A.D., the great silk route had been established for several hundred years. It passed through the southern Caucasus, bringing a steady exchange of art and ideas between the Far East and the Western hemisphere. Invaders had penetrated into the Caucasus through this north-south corridor from Derbend to Baku since the second millenium B.C., contributing with each successive wave to the wealth of ethnic groups who settled in this mountainous range.

More than three hundred distinct ethnic groups have survived until recent times in the remote regions of the Caucasus, a long-time refuge of peoples pushed out of more fertile or accessible lands. Many of these maintained their traditional identities and expressed them in their highly characteristic rug styles. The Circassians, Chechens, Lesghis, Persians, Kurds, and Armenians were best known for their skill at weaving rugs with strong personal designs. The Armenians, settling in this area as far back as the sixth century B.C., were one of the earliest groups praised for their rug making, a tradition which persisted through the invasions of Khazars, Huns, and Avars. By the thirteenth century, the Seljuk Turks succeeded in dominating most of Asia Minor and the Caucasus, which remained in Turkish hands until the seventeenth century. It is therefore no coincidence that animal representations in many Caucasian rugs bear close resemblance to Seljuk designs seen in bronzes of the twelfth century.

The
Caucasus

Plate 26
MAMELUKE, 16' x 11'
wool, 16th Cent.
A very old rug of the type that were produced throughout the Mameluke Empire. A similar rug sold at auction in London in 1978 for $278,000.

The oldest surviving Caucasian rugs—the famed Dragon carpets—date from the mid-sixteenth century. Now mostly in museums, these rare pieces feature large lozenge compartments shaped like highly stylized Far Eastern dragons. Fanciful phoenixes and other small animal figures depicted in brilliant blues, reds, and golds fill the compartments. A Persian influence can be seen in some of the later Dragon carpets, a probable result of the Persian conquest of the Caucasus in the seventeenth century. This conquest led to the division of the Caucasus into fifteen semi-independent Khanates (districts ruled by Khans), such as Gendje and Kuba Karabagh, important rug-weaving districts. During this period, Caucasian weavers incorporated many more naturalistic Persian floral designs into their rugs. The impact of Persia can still be seen in the nineteenth-century Karabagh based on this earlier type, with delightful rows of "maternal" flowers on a navy field (plate 66).

Weaving
in
Europe

In the West, the large and varied output of knotted and woven rugs may be traced to Near Eastern origins, beginning with the earliest workshops in Phoenicia. Over the centuries, three chief trade routes emerged: The great dyeing and weaving centers of antiquity sent their products and techniques to the West through North Africa and Spain, Eastern Europe and Scandinavia, and, of great importance since the thirteenth-century Crusades, Venice.

Coptic textiles may have given the original impetus to the earliest known weaving center in Western Europe, at Chinchilla in Spain. After the Moorish conquest of Spain in the twelfth century, a continuum of Islamic culture ensured the spread of the decorative arts from one end of the Mediterranean to the other, via North Africa. Another offshoot of rug weaving from the Near East came through the Balkans to Eastern Europe and Scandinavia. In more recent centuries, Venetian export and import resulted in a voluminous interchange between Europe and the Orient. By the fifteenth century, the paintings of Hans Holbein vividly testify to the popularity of Turkish rugs, which proliferated in churches, palaces, and wealthy homes. Turkish techniques were introduced into France and England. The Savonnerie workshop was founded in 1628, marking the beginning of the great European looms: Aubusson and Gobelin in France; Norwich, Mortlake, Wilton, and Axminster in England; Madrid in Spain. Some of these looms are active to this day.

Plate 27
SERAPI, 12′4″ x 9′8″
wool, late 19th Cent.
A classic example with the medallion design.

It was in Europe that Oriental rugs were first studied methodically in the nineteenth century, with Wilhelm von Bode, Ernest Kuhnel, Alois Riegl, and Arthur Upham Pope leading the way. Many major scholars of the twentieth century poured their zeal as collectors into important studies, most notably the work of Arthur Urbane Dilley, Joseph V. McMullan, Maurice S. Dimand, Kurt Erdmann, and Cecil Edwards. This scholarship helped to organize major exhibitions, from the first important Oriental rug exhibition in Vienna in 1891 to the more recent shows at the Textile Museum in Washington, D.C.

While many truly rare rugs are in the hands of private collectors, most major museums have at least a few important pieces on exhibition.

Dating Oriental rugs is not an easy task. Rug weaving is a broad and complex field, singularly poor in documentation. A few records exist of conditions in the royal looms of Persia and Turkey, but most rugs were made by illiterate weavers who often copied dates from cartoons as part of the design. So, although Islamic rugs occasionally bear dates, these probably are not accurate. Besides, any conversion system must be used with considerable caution: in the 1920s, many Islamic countries adopted the Western calendar; even before that, in the nineteenth century, the solar calendar was used from time to time, especially in the Caucasus. In addition, to suit the requisites of the design, numbers are occasionally woven backwards.

The traditional Arabic system of dating started in 622 A.D., beginning with the flight of Mohammed from Mecca. It is based on the lunar year, which is longer than the Western solar year: the lunar year gains one solar year every 33.7 solar years. To convert an Islamic date, divide the date by 33.7. Then subtract from the Arabic date, 622 minus $\frac{\text{Arabic Date}}{33}$. If the Arabic date appears in Arabic numerals, it usually reads from left to right, with the following Western equivalents.

10	9	8	7	6	5	4	3	2	1
١٠	٩	٨	٧	٦	٥	٤	٣	٢	١

Besides dates, the continuous tradition of copying older patterns has further complicated attribution of Oriental rugs. Scholars and dealers alike constantly disagree on nomenclature. Trade names are often misleading as an indication of the place where the rug was made—such as Princess Bokhara rugs, which were made neither for royalty nor in the town of Bokhara. The name is used by the trade to suggest prestige and fine quality.

Plate 28
SHIRVAN, 5'5" x 3'5"
wool, 1900
Shirvan weave with Kuba type borders, dated 1317 (1900 A.D.)

CHAPTER III

MATERIALS

Many factors determine the quality of wool, the material used most predominantly in rugs, often forming the sole constituent of the foundation and pile. The breed of sheep, age of the animal, season of shearing, the part sheared, climate, altitude, vegetation, processing—all have a role in defining the texture, thickness, and even the color, of the wool. The mountain breeds of sheep have longer fleeces; spring shearing yields softer and finer wool, while thicker, heavier wool is from winter fleece. Lamb's wool from the eighth to the fourteenth month makes some of the finest wool, called Kork, related to Manchester wool. This type of wool, very thick and silky, was used in Manchester, England. In the late nineteenth and early twentieth centuries, this special breed of sheep was brought to Persia and used for the finest weaving. Skin wool—wool shorn from a dead animal—tends to dry out, lose its sheen, and absorb color less readily.

Camel hair occurs fairly often in certain tribal rugs, such as Kurdish and Beluchi pieces. The outer coat of the camel grows thicker and warmer, while hair from the underbelly tends to be finer. Hamadan and Serab runners use camel hair for durability.

Goat hair appears occasionally in the warp threads of Turkoman rugs and in the selvedges of Beluchis. The soft and beautiful wool of Angora goats crops up in Turkish rugs, while certain very fine Persian rugs make use of Pashmina, a wool from the wild mountain goat (plate 1).

The preparation of the wool makes a great difference to the appearance of the final product. Shearing, done by the men, assures the maximum length of fiber. The fibers are then washed, and sorted for length and coarseness. Then the wool is teased and carded to separate and fluff the fibers, as well as to comb them out, and the long bunches of fibers are ready to be spun on a drop spindle or a spinning wheel. In nomadic and village cultures, weavers often handspin the wool. After spinning, the yarn is ready to be dyed.

Plate 29
SHIRVAN, 5′5″ x 3′5″
wool, early 20th Cent.
Each horse in this piece carries the date 1323 (1906 A.D.).

The use of cotton originated in India and Egypt, although until recently it was rarely employed. Because of its strength, cotton has seen increasing use as warp and weft, and even as pile. Occasionally it surfaces as white areas of the design in Turkoman rugs and kilims. "Polished" cotton is produced by the addition of alkali solutions, which yield a silky effect. It is also called mercerized cotton, after John Mercer who invented the process in the first half of the nineteenth century.

Silk, occurring in rare and expensive pieces, has been cultivated for centuries in China. It is much admired for its resilience, beauty, and luster, and it allows an extreme fineness of weave. Silk was often used in Turkish court prayer rugs. Unfortunately, warm, humid conditions can bring about dry rot, which disintegrates the ground structure and knotting of silk rugs. Also, color tends to be more fugitive in silk rugs.

Most of the rugs seen today contain synthetic and natural dyes. The artificial dyes have been developed over the last century and fall into two groups, aniline and chrome, while the ancient art of natural dyes employs vegetable, animal, and mineral sources.

DYES/COLORS

The use of natural dyes can be traced back to antiquity, when the Phoenicians developed the famous and costly purple dyes of Tyre and Sidon. They derived this dye from shellfish, and long reserved it for royalty. The art of dyeing has had a traditional mystery and prestige—many of the formulas were carefully guarded and handed down through families. The "boyadji" (master of dyes) in many locations of the Near East and as far East as Bokhara held a highly respected position. The boyadji assisted in the entire process, from mordanting the skeins of wool to make it receptive to color, to the dyeing, which took place in boiling vats. The varying local conditions, the small size and unevenness of dye lots, contribute to the many different shades of the same color, called "abrash", or color variation. In earlier times this was thought to be a defect, but lately collectors have come to see abrash as a desirable quality in rugs made with old traditional dyes. The fastness of the natural dyes varies a great deal, but usually, if well applied, the colors undergo a gentle mellowing over the years.

Natural Dyes

Plate 30
BIDJAR KILIM, 6'6" x 4'6"
wool flatweave, mid 19th Cent.
Bidjar is known for its sturdy rugs, but the few kilims they made are the finest.

A considerable range of natural materials have been used for dyeing. The two most common agents were madder for reds and indigo for blues. Madder, extracted from roots of a three- to nine-year-old plant grown ubiquitously over the Near East and Central Asia, provides a rich spectrum of reds from pale brick red to deep plum. The process takes one to two days of soaking the skeins of wool (previously boiled in an alum mordant) in a solution of dried and ground madder root. The colors produced hold very fast to light and washing.

Cochineal, a more bluish red, was derived from two different sources. One early variety came from dried and crushed insects found in the Indian Lac tree, hence the name Lac (or Kermes) for this lasting, preservative carmine dye often seen in earlier Kerman and Khorassan rugs. Another variety of cochineal, introduced from Mexico in the nineteenth century, yielded a more brilliant purple, crimson, scarlet, or, when mixed with madder, cherry pink. Perhaps the vaunted "Turkish red" was such a mixture, as its precise origin and composition have eluded the grasp of scholars.

Blues have been extracted from the indigo plant exported from India. A great variety of hues were obtained after a complex fermentation of indigo mixed with clay, slaked lime, sugar, and potash. Indigo, unlike other dyes, darkens with age or exposure to air. After 1880, a synthetic indigo, closely resembling the natural substance, came into use.

Saffron produces the brightest and most expensive yellow, which therefore limits its use. A milder yellow was obtained from weld, extracted from a vine of the reseda family. Sumac, turmeric, and pomegranate rind also provide various yellows. Greens could be mixed from a bath of indigo followed by a bath of yellow dye. Buckthorn was the yellow most favored by dyers of the Caucasus. A plant long used for dyeing human hair and skin, henna supplies a rich orange as in, for example, the dyed reddish beards of pilgrims returned from Mecca.

White, black, and brown come from natural wool color, but dyes of these colors are obtained with difficulty, especially black. This color could be produced only after steeping the wool in an iron oxide solution, making the wool brittle and subject to rapid wear. In some older rugs, the black areas

Plate 31
SENNEH KILIM, 7' x 5'6"
wool flatweave, late 18th Cent.
Kilims are still woven by Kurdish artists in Sanadaj;
this is a very fine early example.

have completely disappeared, resulting in a sculptural effect. Brown is obtained from a walnut husk or a gall nut base. A bath in madder also achieves a reddish brown. Sometimes even natural colored wool requires special treatment, bleaching in the case of white wool, for example.

The invention of the first aniline dye in 1856 marked a new age in Oriental rug coloring. These acid, coal-tar derivative dyes made the wool stiffer and drier, and the colors tended to run and fade. The earliest aniline dyes produced a mauve and two magentas; the introduction of azo dyes followed in 1864, and alizarin reds came into use about the same time. Late in the nineteenth century, rug aficionados clamored against poorly fixed synthetic dyes, with the result that severe laws restricting their use were enacted in Persia. Synthetic dyes gradually became perfected and consequently dominate modern rug dyeing, except for periods during the two world wars, when rugs briefly returned to natural dyes because of the unavailability of synthetics.

After 1940, the latest and most effective generation of synthetics made their appearance in the form of chrome dyes. Chrome dyes, using potassium bichromate for mordant, come in a wide range of rich colors fast to water, alkali, and sunlight. However, chrome dyes give solid areas of color unrelieved by abrash. Moreover, there is no sign that chrome dyes age at all. Instead, they retain a somewhat harsh brightness.

This strident quality of synthetic colors gave rise to the practice of chemical washing, most commonly seen in Mahal and Sarouk carpets exported to the United States in the 1920s and in Kerman rugs of the 1960s. The strong reds in these carpets were bleached to milder rose tones, which were occasionally painted by hand to a more somber maroon shade. This and other peculiarities of synthetic dyes makes it possible for the connoisseur to date rugs of the last century. For example, a bright orange or magenta faded to gray or brown in a Caucasian rug suggests that the piece was made in the last quarter of the nineteenth century.

TECHNIQUES OF WEAVING

The basic formula for making rugs has certain variations, but essentially the technology has been unchanged for centuries. Pile rugs are made according to the ancient method which combines weaving and knotting. On a

Plate 32
DHURRIE (INDIA), 9′4″ x 6′3″
silk and precious metal thread, c. 1930
Probably made for European or American clients during the Art Deco period.

Pile
Rugs

grid of warp threads stretched on a loom, several shoots of weft are passed from side to side to form a plain weave, or kilim, foundation. The weaver then ties a series of knots, leaving the ends extending on the front side of the rug to form the pile. Rows of knots then alternate with one or more shoots of weft which are beaten down with a comb to produce a dense and sturdy fabric. Then the extending ends of the knots are evenly clipped to form a smooth, thick surface.

The wool or cotton warp runs along the length of the rug. This yarn must be tightly spun to produce a strong weave for the foundation. The wefts pass from side to side and may be loosely spun yarn. They run over and under the warps and pass around the outermost warp cables to form a selvedge. When the rug is removed from the loom, the warp ends may be left as a loose fringe, or they may be braided in a variety of ways depending on the locality.

Flat-weaves

Kilims, or flat-woven rugs, employ even simpler and more ancient techniques than pile rugs. Essentially, a kilim is a rug without knots to form a pile—that is, warp and weft alone. Weft threads of various colors delineate the pattern, and where these threads of different colors meet, they form a small slit, hence the name "slit-weave tapestry." A variant of this technique, called the Soumak weave, involves passing over four warps, then back under two. Whereas kilims can be reversible, soumaks are not, since loose weft threads dangle from the back of the patterns. Verneh and sileh are names for other local variants of flat-weave techniques.

Knotting

Knotting is actually a misnomer for the way the pile is threaded after each row of wefts. Several types of knots are used, although the names don't necessarily reflect the actual locations of usage; some weaving centers use both. The Ghiordes, or Turkish, knot collars two adjacent warps and the pile end emerges between them. The Senneh or Persian knot wraps around one warp with the yarn passing behind the adjacent warp so that a single warp divides the two ends. The Turkish knot is also known as the symmetrical knot; the Persian as the asymmetrical. The Turkish knot, gripping the warp threads more firmly, is sturdier than the Persian knot; however, the technique produces a slightly less fine effect. The Turkish knot occurs in Turkey, the Caucasus, Turkestan, and in Persia used by Turkish or Kurdish weavers. The

Plate 33
SOUMAK, 7'7" x 6'2"
wool flatweave, modern
Soumaks are now being woven in the Soviet Union using designs of historic pieces.

Senneh
Knot

Turkish
Knot

Persian knot appears in Persia, India, Turkestan, Egypt, and in the Turkish court rugs. Spanish rugs use a special knot of their own, looped around single alternate warps with the ends brought out on either side. Finally, the jufti knot, sometimes adopted in east Persia, is tied around four warps, a time-saving process yielding a weaker product.

The simplest loom, that of the nomads, consists of two beams staked to the ground, with the warp stretching taut between them. A shedding device separates alternate warps, so that the weft may pass easily between them. The weaver usually squats in front of the loom, or may sit on a plank supported by two stones on either side of the work in progress. In case of storm, or if the tribe moves on, this horizontal loom may be dismantled quite easily. This type of loom limits the size of rugs to a width of four or five feet.

There are several types of upright looms, used in villages and in town workshops, that enable the weaver to work at eye level or to make larger carpets. One type has a fixed upper beam and a moveable lower cloth beam which fits into slots in the vertical side-pieces. Another, called the Tabriz loom, features adjustable warps wound around the top of the frame, so that the rug may be shifted and pulled down around the back of the loom. The roller-beam loom is a more modern type, used mostly in Turkey. Its two moveable beams allow the rug to be rolled up as work progresses.

The weaver requires only a few simple tools: an iron comb packs down each row of wefts; a knife with a small hook at one end cuts the yarn once the knot is tied; a pair of shears trims the pile. Traditionally, the art of weaving has been passed from mother to daughter. In larger workshops, the weaving proceeds under the guidance of a master (Ma'allem) who knows scores of patterns by heart and calls them out in a chant. Often children are employed in the workshops, although this practice is now forbidden in Iran. As the average rate of production depends on the fineness of the rugs and the weavers' skill, it varies considerably. One set of figures may be taken as a rough guideline: 1,400 knots per day will produce about one square meter in four months.

Despite the wealth of designs introduced over thousands of years and their regional adaptations, several basic formats dominate Oriental rug

Looms

BASIC
DESIGNS

Plate 34
SOUMAK RUNNER, 10'2" x 4'10" ──────
wool flatweave, 19th Cent.
A very fine piece with a rare gold-yellow in the field,
similar to plate 120 in Schurmann's *Caucasian Rugs*.
Plate 35
HAMADAN CAMELHAIR RUNNER, 9'9" x 3'5" ──────
wool and camelhair, early 20th Cent.
The Hamadan and Serab areas are known for these rugs
which use distinctive camelhair wool.

weaving. The most common format is a border and a field. The woven medium itself may have determined this type, as weaving often requires different treatment of the ends and sides to seal the foundation. On another level, in the same way that a frame serves a painting, the border of a rug sets off a sacred or special place. This would be in keeping with the role of rugs in prayer and in association with royal and holy personages, but gradually the border was adopted as a standard artistic tool to emphasize and decorate the enclosed design.

Usually rugs are surrounded by multiple borders. Major borders are those which contain a variant of the central motif, or dominate the other borders in size, or quality and detail of workmanship. The so-called minor borders tend to depict simpler or more standard motifs, functioning in turn as frames for the larger borders. Certain borders imitate architecture, such as the palace window or the mihrab. In this case, the enclosed field becomes a representation of the sky or a garden.

The field may feature allover garden designs with floral clusters arranged symmetrically in space, or a tight grid may be established. Frequently a medallion dominates the center, with minor medallions or portions of the central medallion design repeated in the corners of the rug. In pictorial rugs, the central field contains hunting scenes, animals, the tree of life, vase, or fountain motifs, as well as historic narratives and, occasionally in the twentieth century, commemorative portraits.

Western perspective in such scenes is largely ignored. Instead, symmetry plays a major role in the organization of a design treated more or less freely in motifs, often featuring floral and animal designs, which reached their apogee in Persian weaving; and geometric patterns, which flourished in tribal rugs. The curvilinear designs tend to represent natural forms; the geometric treatment leads to more abstract representations. The selection of pattern originally depends on provenance and will consequently be dealt with in each of the successive chapters. In addition, a glossary at the back of this volume provides specific details of designs used. However, with mass production and the great increase in export trade, many designs began to be used outside their place of origin and were frequently adapted to Western taste, making design alone an inadequate criterion for judging the place of manufacture.

Plate 36
AFSHAR, 5'8" x 4'
wool, kilim ends, early 20th Cent.
Similar to the designs of Caucasian rugs by a tribe that makes few rugs.

The majority of investors buy rugs for decorative and functional purposes. Although rugs have always been symbols of luxury, wealth, and prestige, they have been prized for purely practical reasons. The early tribal rug—one of the most ancient weaving traditions—was small, woven on narrow looms, provided warmth and protection against the harsh elements, and served as floor and wall covers, bags, blankets and cushions. Its small size and design made it easy to transport and readapt to each new setting. Rugs have been used everywhere, from nomadic tent to the floors of the great mosques, from the intimacy of the bedroom to the corporate boardroom. Today designers are rediscovering the versatility of handmade rugs—their wealth of designs and their multiple uses.

Although wall-to-wall carpeting and machine-made rugs dominated the market in the 1950s and 1960s, the seventies have seen a return to Oriental rugs. Unlike wall-to-wall carpeting, which is short-lived and difficult to uproot, rugs are lasting and flexible—they can be rolled up in the summer and reused in new contexts. In contrast to machine-made rugs, Orientals can be sold when the owner needs to move, or becomes tired of the piece.

Modern architects and interior designers are learning how to use rugs to organize space. Rugs work as room dividers without creating physical barriers. In a large, unmodified area—a loft or a large living room—small rugs break up the space to define living or working spaces. Even in the restricted space of the Sutton Place living room featured here, rugs divide without creating an impression of crowding or disruption (see plate 40). Here, the color and classic geometric design of the Oriental rugs have unified the antique and contemporary furniture to create a harmonious mix. By leaving space between the wall and floor, the architect produces an effect of space and light. The rich coloration of the rugs draws attention away from the low ceilings to increase the apparent height of the room. Fine rugs add focus and drama to a grouping of furniture, articulate space, and enhance the architecture. The modulations of design in Oriental rugs solve the monotonous problems of elegant lobbies and reception rooms.

Plate 37
BAKHTIARI, 23′5″ x 15′9″
wool, early 20th Cent.
An unusual large tribal piece.

84

Above all, interior designers have recognized that fine rugs can create a variety of moods, as well as meet practical needs. Decorators point out that the thick pile wool rugs, with brilliant coloration, such as Kazaks, Shirvans, or other Caucasian rugs create a feeling of warmth. They are versatile enough to fit into informal settings or to produce a theatrical effect. Similarly, Oushaks and Agras work in classically traditional environments and casual interiors. The light pastel colored Oushaks, favored in warm climates and summer homes, can suggest a cool, summery open and relaxed effect. In plate 39 the salmon colored nineteenth-century piece gives a distinctive spacious effect in combination with the simple lines of contemporary furniture and art work. An Oushak with a similar color scheme and design integrates equally well with period French furniture (see plate 41). The muted subtleties of the Oushak work well with the rich and delicate lines of eighteenth-century salon pieces. Heriz, Serapis and many nineteenth-century Chinese rugs offer a similar flexibility in adapting to modern and antique furniture without overpowering the exisiting decor or art work.

Large Sarouks, Serapis, Kermans, and Isfahans, which have become more readily available on the market with the construction of smaller interiors in the seventies, are well adapted to the lobbies of elegant hotels and international banks. Smaller classic rugs, such as Kashans, Sarouks, Ferahans, Herekes, and Qums have traditionally been used in libraries, living rooms, and parlors with French and English furniture, particularly in areas where they are not overexposed to wear. Exceptionally fine and delicate pieces have been hung as tapestries, often with an opulent and luxurious effect.

The bold Turkoman and Caucasian rugs, with their masculine geometric designs have appealed to doctors and other professionals with a marked regard for individuality. They have been placed in libraries, foyers and offices.

Alternative
Uses

As traditional floor coverings, Oriental rugs introduce a note of originality and distinction into the home or office. Innovative designers have used rugs as hangings over balconies, as table tops pressed under glass or lucite, as cushion and sofa covers. Several corporate art curators and architects, given the comparatively lower cost of rugs as art in relation to secondary masters in

Plate 38
SAROUK, 14′8″ x 10′6″
wool, early 20th Cent.
A Mahajeran Sarouk with a "Gul Farang" design, very similar to rugs from Bidjar.

painting, have elected to hang fine rugs in boardrooms and executive offices. Several major hotels, such as the United Nations Plaza in New York and the Hyatt Regency in Boston, are displaying mounted antique textiles throughout their public spaces with striking verve and elegance. This is but another example of the infinite variety of uses for the woven arts.

Many people believe that cleaning may damage a rug, yet proper care removes the dirt, conditions the fibers, and may prolong the life of your rug. Traditionally, in many parts of the Middle East, rugs were washed in local streams with heavy soap and left to dry in the sun, or, in winter, were turned face down on the snow and vigorously beaten. Although this process led to a gentle mellowing of the colors, much appreciated by collectors, it often dehydrated the fibers, weakened the structure, and caused certain of the dyes to bleed. Cleaning techniques have improved, and can actually prolong the life of your rug. Too often, however, rug owners either attempt to clean the rugs themselves or do not seek the best professional advice and services.

Several steps may be taken at home to assure the long life and beauty of your rug. A foam rubber pad at least 3/8″ thick should be placed under the rug to prevent slippage, and to safeguard against wear caused by the friction of the rug against a hard surface. Such pads are available from most fine dealers at a low cost. Whenever possible, it is preferable to place a fine rug in a low traffic area. To assure even wear, many collectors periodically turn their rugs around. Obviously, in the case of very fine silks or rare or damaged rugs of great age, hanging or mounting will prolong the life of such pieces. When hanging a rug or tapestry, avoid hooks and nails which may puncture or pull the foundations or result in scalloping. A pole strung through a backing or velcro tape will allow for a more even distribution of the suspended weight. All rugs, including those you might have hanging, collect dust and should be vacuumed with the air draft hose. Vacuuming on both sides of rugs removes more of the dirt. To protect the rug, avoid over-vacuuming. Any animal spot or stain should be taken care of immediately with plain cold water applied in the soiled area to avoid spreading harmful substances. I recommend to have paper towels handy to mop up any excess water. If neglected, the spot will become impossible to remove.

CARE & RESTORATION

Home Care

Plate 39 (top)
INTERIOR _____
Photo by Ernest Silva, New York
A lovely Agra, India rug subtly unifies this modern setting.
Plate 40 (Below)
INTERIOR _____
Photo by Thomas Feist, New York
A large Serapi and Chila (foreground) add life and
color to this contemporary interior.

Professional
Care

I have often seen valuable rugs severely damaged by home shampooing. Many commercial rug shampoos dehydrate the pile and fail to clean in depth. It is difficult to dry rugs adequately at home, and damp may promote decay. I suggest that every year, or in some cases every two years, rugs should be sent to a cleaning specialist (several of which are listed in the back of this book). I am sometimes startled to find that a collector, after taking great pains to select a piece, will assume that the cleaner who handles his silk shirt can clean his silk kashan. Specialized cleaning of valuable antiques is almost an art in itself. It requires familiarity with the materials, weaves, and dyes of the rugs, and also proper space, chemicals, and equipment to treat them. Many recognized cleaners will follow a basic four-point procedure. (1) They surface-clean the rug and determine condition and dye fastness. (2) They apply a series of solutions: an initial surface rub, an immersion bath in a neutral cleaner (dosed according to weight and soilage), a lanolin dispersion agent. This procedure may be repeated several times. (3) The rug is then dried through an air blowing process. (4) In most cases a lanolin solution is then reapplied to restore luster and to avoid dehydration of the fibers.

Restoration

Many cleaning specialists and fine rug dealers operate restoration workshops as well (see list). It takes the eye of an expert to assess the type and extent of the damage. Trained restorers can reconstruct the foundation and reweave the pile (a slow and expensive procedure), sew tears, coil selvedges, and repair and replace borders. Surface techniques, performed on lesser pieces or where damage is too extensive, include patching and touching (painting). A good repair job will not only enhance the appearance of your piece, but will protect it from further damage. The client should allow for considerable restoration time, as the process is often long and painstaking.

Plate 41
INTERIOR
Photo by Ernest Silva, New York
An Oushak rug quietly complements period furniture
and appointments.

CHAPTER IV

Oriental rugs are most often associated with Persia because the lion's share of rugs exported to the West in the nineteenth and early twentieth centuries came from there. The superb quality of Persian wools and silks, dyes composed in harmonious shades, and the long tradition of master craftsmanship have earned these rugs their reputation as the finest examples of the knotted art. Their rich variety of patterns and remarkable number of weaves makes it difficult to generalize about materials and techniques (both the Senneh and Ghiordes knots are used throughout Persia, sometimes in the same region). Yet despite the wealth of types, Persian rugs are highly distinctive. They impress us with the formality of their elegant designs; they favor curvilinear floral motifs and crisp, symmetrically arranged medallions on fields surrounded by several borders. The intricate detail expressed by flowing curves is at once distinguishable from the more geometric devices used on the neighboring rugs of Turkey and the Caucasus.

The traditional Persia of rug weaving occupied a pivotal position among the rug-producing countries, with Turkey to the west, the Caucasus to the north, and Turkestan to the east. At her zenith in the seventeenth century, Persia encompassed the territory of the Safavid Empire, which stretched beyond present-day Iran to include parts of Western Afghanistan, Soviet Azerbaijan, Iraq, and Syria. This land rises to form a vast plateau reaching an elevation of roughly four thousand feet in Western Asia, bordered to the north by the massive chains of the Elborz and to the southeast by the Zagros mountains. For the most part the great plain is an arid steppe, broken by flowering oases. It is not surprising that Persians delighted in the traditional theme of the garden, often associating such places with Paradise; the word for Paradise in Persian is "Beshetht," meaning walled garden. The flowering garden theme, along with many other famous patterns such as the Herat, the Guli Hinani, and the Mina Khani, became popular in the sixteenth and seventeenth centuries and are still strikingly in evidence on many Persian rugs today.

PERSIAN RUGS

Plate 42
SERAPI, 12'8" x 9'4"
wool, c. 1900
A fine Serapi with an unusual garden design.
(Property of a European Investment Firm)

By the latter half of the nineteenth century, an increased surge in Western demand for Oriental rugs brought a fresh emergence of city workshop production, starting with Tabriz in the 1860s. Merchants in the export centers of Kerman, Khorassan, Sultanabad, Kashan, Hamadan, Bidjar, Ferahan, and Heriz soon followed the trend. Foreign firms opened their own factories, such as Petag in Tabriz and Ziegler in Sultanabad. They strictly controlled colors, designs, and weaving for the foreign market. But some weavers and designers did not follow the changes dictated. Although they accepted commissions, their style was so exceptional that, even when no signature exists in the rug, the work of an individual master is recognizable. Such proverbial hallmarks of the modern period are the Mohtasham Kashan, the Dabir Kashan, the Hadji Jalili Tabriz, and the Amoghli Mashad (plates 10,11,12,13). Occasionally, European and American buyers had their company names knotted into rugs. The best known of these are Costigian, Ghastili, Dilmaghani of Kerman, and Tafshanchian of Arak.

A typical example of Western influence and trade patterns may be seen in the recent history of Sarouk rugs. In the 1880s, this small village responded to the demand made by the European market, via Tabriz merchants, by producing a medallion design in place of the Safavid revival-style rugs of the earlier years. The initially somewhat rectilinear design evolved into more graceful and fluid curves as the weavers learned to work from detailed cartoons. The lag in rug production caused by World War I was followed by an increased demand from the American market, which resulted in a very different product. The delicate color variation of earlier Sarouks was replaced by harsh dyes. This led to the unfortunate practice of bleaching and repainting many of the rugs. Another revival of the rug industry in the 1940s, responding to the rise of the American market and government regulations under Reza Shah Pahlavi, led to somewhat better quality control.

Cecil Edwards's monograph, *The Persian Carpet*, provides a good survey of late-nineteenth- and early twentieth-century Persian rugs. His research has shed a great deal of light on this complex subject. The development of designs in Persia is one of the most complicated of any rug-producing country. The main centers of weaving generated many important and distinct patterns,

Plate 43
ANTIQUE SENNEH, 6′9″ x 4′6″
wool, 19th Cent.
A rare white border distinguishes this otherwise typical example.

which were quickly copied by local offshoots. In turn, these patterns were copied by more distant weaving centers. At the same time, much adaptation and cross-fertilization also went on. Today, patterns originally from one area are used ubiquitously and continue to be readapted to current fashion tastes. This makes any cut-and-dried classification of Persian rug designs somewhat simplistic. In the following brief survey, we shall only deal with the major rug-producing centers by geographic area.

A great variety of rugs have been produced over the last hundred years in the northwest of Persia, in areas historically known as Kurdistan, Azerbaijan, and Armenia. Bidjar, in the Kurdistan region, weaves rugs known for their rich, deep colors and extremely tight, sturdy, long-wearing construction. Their sturdiness is due to multiple filler wefts inserted between rows of knots, which also makes these rugs difficult to fold. The weavers favor large room and corridor sizes in medallion designs and floral repeats, as well as the Western floral pattern called "Gul Farangs".

Bidjar

Senneh rugs are thinner and more pliable because of their often very fine knotting (up to 400 per square inch), thin warp of cotton or silk, and single weft. The backs of these rugs have a rough, sandpapery feel because of the particular single weft crossing of the foundation. Smaller sizes of these rugs with minute floral patterns are favored, in combination with medallion designs (plate 43). The delicate color scale rests on sandy tones, pinks, ivory, and black. Senneh is also famous for its kilims, which are the finest made anywhere (plate 31). It is curious that, although Senneh gave its name to the knot also known as Persian or asymmetrical, many of the rugs woven in the area use the Turkish knot.

Senneh

Hamadan sits in the center of a large rug-producing area with hundreds of villages and more than ten thousand looms. Coarser, longer-pile rugs are made here, including runners framed by a characteristic plain camel border (plate 35). Occasionally, one finds heavy piled, finely knotted rugs in Sarouk designs, called "Kazvin" in America, but they actually come from Hamadan and should bear the name "Hamadan Shahrbaff."

Hamadan

Situated near Hamadan, the town of Malayer produces rugs resembling Sarouks of the older type, but they use the Turkish knot.

Malayer

Plate 44
FERAHAN (MALAYER), 7'4" x 5'3"
wool, late 19th Cent.
An outstanding early example, much sought by collectors.

95

Tabriz

To the northwest, Tabriz, the capital of the old state of Azerbaijan and today the second largest city in Iran, has flourished as a rug center since the fifteenth and sixteenth centuries. Its weavers were repeatedly requisitioned by the sultans of Turkey and the shahs of Persia. Their masterpieces form the heart of many major museum collections today. Modern production may be said to have started when the English firm of Ziegler established factories here in 1885. The German firm of Petag soon followed. Hadji Jalili achieved recognition as the most famous weaver working in Tabriz around the turn of this century. He produced extremely fine versions of historical designs, such as the Ardebil, executed in a pleasing brick red, creamy white, and soft greens (plate 2). Characteristic of Jalili's style are finely knotted medallion designs done in soft colors, occasionally in silk, with short pile and precise drawing (plates 5, 11).

Heriz

Just northeast of Tabriz lies Heriz, know for the most sumptuous silk rugs (plate 3). Wool rugs produced with the same care convey an equal elegance and are much sought by serious collectors. The United States imported many late-nineteenth-century Herizes. These rugs impress us with their crisply designed madallions and dazzling madder, indigo, or ivory fields in large squarish formats, although smaller examples are also found (plate 45).

Serapi is the name given to best grade of Heriz rugs, which have boldly conceived medallion designs in crystalline colors (plates 4, 15,27). Serapis may have cartouches in their borders containing poems and other inscriptions; dignitaries usually commissioned such pieces for special occasions. The coarser, less costly grades from the Heriz area go by the name of Gorevan. The designs of these rugs are similar to the better grades, but the weave is less fine and the colors are harsher.

Bakshaish
Ardebil
Meshkin
Rasht

Bakshaish, another town in the Heriz area, produces many room-size rugs. In recent years, Ardebil and Meshkin have been the source of mass-produced rugs copied from Caucasian designs.

On the Caspian shore, Rasht has been known for a characteristic type of embroidered appliqué work used for coverlets. The Royal Ontario Museum in Toronto owns several excellent specimens.

Plate 45
HERIZ, 12′2″ x 9′3″
This is a typical example of a forty year old Heriz,
erroneously called Serapi by some dealers.

Some of the towns discussed here, namely, Senneh, Bidjar, and Hamadan are located in the region of Kurdistan. In the past, labels such as "Mosul" or "Suj Bulak" were used for Kurdish products. Today, semi-nomadic Kurds produce a number of different rug types, and their utility bags are increasingly prized by collectors. Kurdistan has a reputation for using lustrous wools and traditional vegetable dyes.

The Sarouk region in central Persia has its center at Arak (formerly Sultanabad). In terms of commercial production, Sarouk competes only with the Hamadan region. Following the revival of rug making in the northwest, local manufacturers such as Mahajaran began production for export, usually medallion rugs in rich reds and blues (plate 38). The name "Sarouk" or "Ferahan Sarouk" is reserved for the finer pieces, which have velvety short pile (plate 44). Antique examples usually have medallion centers, with cotton warp and weft. The Sarouks of the 1920-1940 period featured detached overall floral designs on a rose ground. Many of the "painted Sarouks" have been bought up by the German market in recent years (plate 48). The very finest grade of all the Ferahan Sarouks is called "Mahajeran," after an early local manufacturer. These usually have a central medallion on a field of rose and dark red. Yellow guard-stripes flank their wide, midnight-blue borders. Currently, Sarouks of good quality continue to be made under the label of Jozan.

East of Sarouk lies Ferahan, one of the first Persian rug centers to export to the West in the nineteenth century. Ferahan rugs exhibit a unique pistachio or apple green, usually found in the border. This corrosive color has lowered the pile in older examples (plate 14). The overall Herati pattern appears most frequently in these rugs; medallion designs are rarer. The "Moharemati Ferahan" reminds one of Gasghai rugs, but it contains the familiar local pale green (plate 92).

Old Mahal rugs are lighter in weight, and softer and more loosely knotted than Sarouks. Decorators seek them for their subdued colors. The firm of Ziegler started a late-nineteenth-century venture here that led to rugs with a red field carrying the "Gul Hinani" floral repeat, surrounded by a dark blue border with soft greens, and yellow highlights (plate 74).

Plate 46
RAVAR KERMAN, 6'5" x 4'2"
wool, late 19th Cent.
A typical example from this southeast Persian center, made for the European market.

Kashan

Farther south, we come to Kashan, an important and historical rug center; the great Ardebil Carpets were almost certainly woven here in the sixteenth century. Both silk and wool rugs have been made in this center since the nineteenth-century by master craftsmen called "Ustad kar" (plate 47). Probably half of Persia's nineteenth-century silk rugs were made here. For three generations, a family of artisans wove "Mohtashams," the most highly regarded and sought-after rugs. One outstanding pictorial Mohtasham Kashan shows a scene from the *Shah-nameh* (*A King's Book of Kings*, the great masterpiece of Persian miniature painting) (plate 13). Solomon sits in the center, surrounded by his court; the lower part of the rug and the border feature scenes from Rustam's fabled taming of the animals and monsters of the world. Another outstanding Mohtasham Kashan commemorates the conquest of India by Nadir Shah, who is shown with his learned advisors and the crown prince (plate 12). The queen is stylized as the radiant sun, in deference to a tradition against direct depiction of a woman. A border with realistic hunting scenes completes the piece.

Natanz
Haroon
Qum
Nain
Isfahan

Good Kashan rugs of this period were also produced under the name "Dabir." Nearby Natanz and Haroon are known for a lower grade of rugs.

In the last twenty years, Qum and Nain have surfaced with tightly woven rugs, mostly in light colors, as well as fine silks (plate 86).

Isfahan, the great Safavid capital, has also reappeared as a rug producer in the last twenty years. The favorite old themes of central medallions, overall florals, and garden scenes have reemerged today in rugs of high-quality craftsmanship using good wool. The workshop of Serafian now holds the reputation of making the masterpieces of today, with highly realistic floral and animal compositions knotted in the finest weave (plate 8).

Bakhtiari

In contrast to the town and city productivity, the Bakhtiari, southwest of Isfahan, weave village and tribal rugs. They make a characteristic design of rectangular or lozenge compartments containing stylized floral elements with pronounced greens, blues, and ivory (plate 37).

EAST & SOUTH
PERSIA
Khorassan

The eastern province of Khorassan lies adjacent to Afghanistan, with Herat to the east and Turkestan to the north. Here, too, rug making has revived since the 1880s. Mashad, Doroksh, Sarakhs, and Mood produce the majority of rugs in this district.

Plate 47
KASHAN, 6'6" x 4'3"
wool, 20th Cent.
A fine classical piece from a center that continues to produce high quality rugs. This rug recalls the art of the Moghul miniature painters.

Mashad, the capital of Khorassan, is a holy city of shrines, including the shrine of the imam Ali Riza, with its collection of antique rugs (Cecil Edwards's *The Persian Carpet* gives a good description of these). A cochineal red appearing as a deep magenta dominates Mashad rugs. The designs usually follow classical examples of Herati patterns and a paisley originally seen in Kerman shawls from the sixteenth to eighteenth centuries. In the 1900s, the Amoghli workshop of Mashad turned out extraordinarily fine rugs for the court of Reza Shah Pahlavi. A jewel-like example from the author's collection shows an intricate network of curling floral stems on an ivory ground (plate 10).

Mashad

Completing our tour of Persia, we arrive at the city of Kerman, one of the great traditional rug centers where old patterns survived until the late nineteenth century. These older pieces became known as "Laver Kermans," a transformation of the name of the neighboring town of Ravar. Later Kermans, made for the European and American markets, are favored for their lighter shades and pastel colors. The Tree of Life design was often seen, with its rich arrangement of flowering curvilinear branches and birds (plate 88). This recalls the ancient Persian theme of the walled garden, with its overtones of Paradise. Kerman also produced medallion-design rugs (plate 46).

Kerman

Another remarkable product of Kerman weaving was the shawl, closely resembling those woven in Kashmir since the fifteenth century. They were made from rare pashmina wool shorn from the whitest fleece of a Himalayan mountain goat. The shawls, sometimes containing nearly two thousand knots in a square inch, reflect the gem-like craftsmanship and wealth of designs perfected over five centuries. In Kashmir, both men and women wove shawls, but in Kerman, young girls toiled over these pieces from the age of six until they married. It took the combined effort of three or four girls over five years to complete a "taghe" shawl measuring approximately seven by four feet. The shawls are often characterized by a densely ornamented field. A Kerman shawl from the eighteenth century displays a good example of the "mother and baby" boteh motif (plate 102). Here, large botehs are interspersed with smaller inverted botehs. Other popular design motifs include fields of little pomegranate blossoms and buds.

Kerman
Shawls

Plate 48
SAROUK, 7'3" x 4'11"
wool, c. 1925
An untreated piece similar in design to the "wash and paint"
commercial Sarouks of the 1920's.

These shawls attained their height of popularity in Europe, where renowned society ladies, including the empress Josephine of France, coveted these costly and exotic cloaks. English weavers in Paisley and Norwich began to imitate the shawls, as did the weavers of France. To accommodate European demand and taste, this woven art was soon transformed into an industry and deteriorated rapidly. Adulterated mixes replaced the special wools, embroidery replaced weaving. With the end of the Franco-Prussian war, shawls passed out of fashion, and thus ended the shawl trade.

Afshar

Ghashgai

The Afshari tribe lives to the north and west of Kerman. This tribe weaves bright geometric rugs in smaller formats, reminiscent of their origins in Azerbaijan (plates 36, 91). Another, larger, tribal group is the semi-nomadic Ghasghai who speak a Turkic dialect and live in southwest Persia in the province of Fars. They and the less numerous members of the Khamseh Federation market their rugs at Shiraz. Antique Ghasghais are surely among the finest Persian rugs in terms of wool and dye quality (plates 49). In both of these examples, the ivory border with its hooked angular motifs betrays the Turkic origins of the tribe. A panel at each end of Ghasghais, composed of three narrow horizontal stripes divided into rectangular compartments, helps to identify them. The woven and flat-woven saddlebags closely resembles a Beluchi saddlebag in design, with similar stepped polygons in the kilim technique (plate 101). With tribal traditions rapidly disappearing, these artifacts are becoming more and more valuable collectors' items.

* * * * *

Collections

The most important collections of Persian rugs are now at the Metropolitan Museum of Art in New York City, the National Museum of Teheran (a collection assembled by the last shah), and the Boston Museum of Fine Arts. Recently, a major exhibition, *Masterpieces from German Private Collections,* was shown in Munich. These exhibitions brought public attention to an art formerly appreciated only by connoisseurs. Persian rugs have always been collected as examples of the highest art of weaving, and Iran still produces the finest rugs (see Chapter XI), although it has fallen behind in quantity.

Plate 49
GHASHGAI, 7'3" x 5'6"
wool, c. 1880
An unusual "millefleur" design, with a border which
shows Caucasian influence.
Exhibited, Museum of the Philadelphia Civic Center, 1978.

CHAPTER V

From late medieval times until the early nineteenth century, Turkish weaving dominated the Western rug-export trade. In the seventeenth century, Turkish exports were so prevalent that any Oriental rug was called a Turkey carpet. The great variety of Turkish rugs, from the refined silken splendors of Suleiman the Magnificent's court looms to the wool-and-goat-hair homespun mystique of Anatolian village weaving, could suit the diverse requirements of an altarpiece in Flanders and a throw rug in an elegant Venetian boudoir. Turkish weavers incorporated elements of design from the severe rectilinear gridwork of early Seljuk rugs to the curvilinear elegance of classical Persian pieces.

The geographic location at once explains the variety of influence on Turkish rug art: Persia and Armenia on the east, and Europe and Egypt on the west, by sea. The Anatolian peninsula of Turkey juts west from the Near East, and is surrounded by four seas: the Aegean, the Mediterranean, the Sea of Marmara on the south and west, and the Black Sea on the north. This high and arid plateau is most jagged on the east, where Ararat rises over 18,000 feet, an ideal environment for raising sheep.

Traditionally, Turkey made rugs from its native wool, which varied greatly in quality, and until the nineteenth century, rugs were woven almost entirely from this material, including the foundation. Throughout Anatolia, peasant women bred their own silkworms, while the district around Bursa provided the excellent silk for the Hereke rugs. Near the Syrian border, camels provided a coarse but strong wool. The nomadic tribes favored goat hair, which can still be seen in the high-pile Yoruk rugs.

The wools were dyed with many of the standard natural dyes. The weavers favored madder and citric acids for making their rusts and vermilions. The noted golden yellow came primarily from acorns and lye residue, while the light yellow had a lemon base. The characteristic green was derived from the hait plant and copper sulphate, and black was obtained from a delicate mixture of volcanic muds.

TURKISH RUGS

Plate 50
GHIORDES PRAYER, 5'3" x 4'4"
wool, late 18th Cent.
A classical design from the ancient weaving center.

In the nineteenth century, countless rugs were produced for European export. They ranged in quality from the finest Hereke silks to the most barbarized, loosely woven rugs with the poorest quality aniline dyes, following designs dictated by the foreign markets. Traditionally, the Greeks and Armenians wove the finest pieces. Following World War I, the Turks mercilessly persecuted them, forcing the survivors to flee the country in large numbers. Throughout Turkey thousands of peasants still pursue weaving for additional income. Where cottage industry prevails, the rugs tend to be small, in keeping with the height of the hut. Natural dyes are still used in some cases, and there is strong pride in workmanship. Over the last twenty years, the Sumer National Bank has been financing most of the weaving, and provides wool on the barter system. Modern designs borrow from traditional patterns, resulting in an eclectic production.

ISTANBUL DISTRICT

Oushak

The town of Oushak, roughly one hundred miles directly south of Istanbul, produced some of the most commercial rugs of all times. Their distinctive designs appear as early as the fifteenth century in the paintings of Lorenzo Lotto; they are mentioned as part of the booty of the Polish king, John III Sobieski; and they are found in the Savonnerie motifs of the seventeenth century. In the nineteenth century, the traditional deep indigo and vermilion tones of the so-called "Star Oushake" gave way to more subtle earth tones of coral, ivory, gray, and olive green. Frequently used as coverings for the floors of mosques, these large rugs also lent themselves to the export trade. The two rugs shown here exemplify the late-nineteenth and turn-of-the-century Oushaks, whose rough weave and muted coloration appealed to contemporary interior designers (plate 53).

Prayer Rugs

Nothing is more expressive of the Turkish sensibility than an antique Oushak prayer rug, with its crisply outlined stepped prayer niche harking back to Seljuk architecture. Another prayer rug from the eighteenth century, with its curving arch, spandrels studded with undulating arabesques, recalls the floral exuberance of the Safavid seventeenth-century rugs of Persia (plate 24). The prayer rug represents the pinacle of Turkish weaving. Five times a day, the devout kneels on his rug with the arch directed toward Mecca and places a pilgrimage stone at its point. The prayer arch, or mihrab, dominates

Plate 51
SIVAS PRAYER, 6'1" x 4'
wool, late 19th Cent.
This design shows a strong Persian influence on the native style and coloration.

the design. In Anatolian examples, many small devices accompany the mihrab motif, most commonly the lamp, light of Allah, or the ewer, symbol of cleanliness (it is customary for the faithful to wash before prayer). A sevenfold border evokes the seven heavens awaiting the true believer.

To the west of Oushak, in Anatolia, the small towns of Ghiordes and Kula have earned a high regard for their magnificent prayer rugs. At times, they are very difficult to tell apart, although the double weft of Kulas is said to be a differentiating characteristic. Ghiordes rugs usually measure under seven feet, and come in cool color schemes with medallion patterns in addition to prayer-rug designs; for example, a central field that terminates at either end in the shape of a typical stepped prayer arch (plate 6). The spandrels, filled with angular flowers, and the horizontal panels at each end containing floral sprigs characterize the prayer rugs. The silver-gray and heliotrope are again typical of subdued Ghiordes colors. Another example has a similar color scheme, with the traditional prayer arch and floral bouquet suspended over a pale pistachio mihrab (plate 50). The "Kiz Ghiordes" appears in a small, squarish format of a medallion rug with a broad wavy band in the border, and is thought to have been a traditional dowry piece (as were the Bergama Kiz).

Kula rugs frequently have multiple border stripes, usually seven, often featuring the "shobokli," pipe-stem pattern, and only one horizontal panel, as opposed to two in Ghiordes rugs. A characteristic Kula design, "Mezarlik" (cemetery), depicts small repeating arrangements of a house flanked by two cypresses, usually on a dark field. These rugs may have been used by the family to pray for the soul of the departed, and some have been found in tombs.

Hereke rugs derive their name from a village located north of Kula, some forty miles from Istanbul on the Gulf of Ismid. In 1884, the Sultan Abdul Mejid established this old weaving center as a royal factory, commissioning Persian master-weavers to set up the highest quality weaving industry. This resulted in rugs woven entirely of silk, with over a million knots per square yard. The silk Hereke testifies to the heights reached in formal design, betraying Persian inspiration in elegant oval medallions and gracefully

ANATOLIAN RUGS

Ghiordes

Kula

Hereke

Plate 52
HEREKE, 6' 6" x 4'
silk, 18th Cent.
A classic early example from a center that continues
to make the finest Turkish silk rugs.

curling cloud bands and floral sprays (plate 52). This style also appears in one of the world's largest prayer rugs (19' by 16'), probably designed for King Farouk of Egypt in the first decade of the twentieth century (plate 9). The delicate tracery indicates the Persian influence, while the great sheet of old gold set off by the red detail characterizes Anatolian use of color. These rugs catered to the Western market in the second half of the nineteenth century, and incorporated Savonnerie motifs and heraldic insignia with elaborate encrustations of gold and silver brocade. Today, in the hands of the Sumer National Bank, Hereke continues to produce the highest quality rugs.

Melas

Melas, on the southwest coast of Turkey in Western Anatolia, has a long tradition of making prayer rugs warmly colored in reds, yellows, and aubergine. The prayer arch is usually pinched in by two triangular wedges near the top. A very unusual example of this type resembles the Kula in its design, especially the spandrels filled with flower heads and the two columns containing floral stems, but its unmistakable color scheme and red wefts identify it as a Melas (plate 25). Another type from this region, often called "Karaova melas," consists of vertical panels carrying an angular stem meander with cockscomb-like attachments and turtle medallions.

Ladik

Konya

Ladik and Konya, in Central Anatolia, both draw on a long history of rug making. Ladik ranks especially high in the pantheon of Anatolian prayer rugs. Earlier types included the triple-arch-and-column prayer rug. Later examples from the late eighteenth century are known for their blazing reds and clear blues articulating an open field and horizontal panels with slender tulips among the crenelations or vandykes of what looks like a battlement. Konya rugs feature a looser weave and a more subdued color spectrum in earth shades of brown, beige, dull yellows, and reds.

Makri

The village of Makri (Fethiye) in southern Anatolia also produced brilliant prayer rugs with two vertical panels of differing colors, containing large geometric devices in strong yellows, blues, and reds, with a predominance of ivory. These colors resemble those of certain Caucasian rug types.

Bergama

Up the coast from Makri rises the hilly Bergama region. This region is famous for many types of rugs, mostly of a smaller size, under eight by six

Plate 53
OUSHAK, 16'2" x 13'3"
wool, late 19th Cent.
This rug is of an unusual color and distinctive design.
(Private Collection, Virginia)

feet. The boldly geometric patterns recall Caucasian Kazak designs (plate 54). Some of the finest Bergama rugs are the "Kiz," or wedding rugs, traditionally woven by the bride to commemorate the great event of her life. The field usually contains a hexagonal medallion and stars, with a wavy band running along the broad border. The favorite colors are yellow, sand, apricot, and light blue in delicate harmonies, giving these rugs a "peaches and cream" aura.

Kirshehir and Mudjur, villages in central Anatolia, produced their share of outstanding prayer rugs with characteristic color schemes. Kirshehir favored a cherry-red or magenta field accented by aqua, light green, or blue—a far cry from modern examples with harsh synthetic colors. Mudjur rugs sometimes employed as many as a dozen different colors, yet maintained a sparkling clarity of tone. A mosaic-like effect is produced by the delicately worked main borders articulated into square compartments containing angular flowers in a diamond pattern. These rugs are still available, but the supply is diminishing. *Kirshehir*

Mudjur

Sivas, located near the Persian border in eastern Anatolia, borrowed many color and design schemes from Tabriz. The tight weave and rich earth tones of Tabriz appear in the Sivas rug in plate 51. *Sivas*

Also influenced by Persia, Angora rugs borrowed many motifs such as the boteh for its fine rugs, woven in the famed Angora goat hair. *Angora*

A few traditional Anatolian village rug types are surrounded by a sea of less easily identifiable rugs also meriting the label "Anatolian." In addition to the settled peasant population, a large number of nomads, frequently of Kurdish descent, roam the hills and valleys of Asia Minor and go by the collective name of Yuruk. The shaggy, boldly conceived, and coarsely knotted Yuruk rugs, with braided ends and mostly in smaller sizes, provide insulation for the tents of these wanderers. Bright colors, chiefly magenta, green, and deep blue, ivory, and a variety of natural browns form the palette of these primitive and durable rugs (plate 55). *Anatolian Village Rugs*

Anatolia has prided itself on a long tradition of flat-weaves. The patterns favor extreme geometric designs that conform to the limitations of the technique. Kilims serve as hangings, coverlets, and prayer mats. Of the large *Flat-weaves*

Plate 54
BERGAMA, 5'6" x 4'2"
wool, kilim ends, early 20th Cent.
Many of the features of this rug show Caucasian influences.

115

variety produced, most are prayer kilims and long kilims, usually twelve to fourteen feet long, woven in two strips and sewn together afterwards. Anatolian kilims have been receiving more attention since the publication of *The Undiscovered Kilim* by Black and Loveless, and *Kilims* by Y. Petsopoulos. A related flat-weave type, called cicim (djidjim) is also used for curtains and coverlets. Cicim are embroidered or brocaded kilims, with the loose ends of the weft-face embroidery pattern hanging free in the back.

. . . . .

Scholarship

The wools, dyes, and designs of Turkish rugs are the most studied, mainly because they have been part of European trade for so many centuries, and partly because there are more of them left to study. In Turkey, more so than in any other country, administrators of the mosques treasured the rugs woven for their sanctuaries and carefully preserved them there. And in the sixteenth century, the Ottomans, to teach the cartoonists and instill in them a sense of excellence, collected numerous examples of the finest rugs and kept them in the royal museums. Exhibitions such as *Masterpieces from German Private Collections*, with its lavish catalogue entitled *Old Eastern Carpets, masterpieces in German Collections*, and the reprint of *Tapis Turcs* in 1977 have stimulated international interest in Turkish rugs. This is reflected in the rising prices of antique and semi-antique Turkish pieces.

Plate 55
YORUK, 7'2" x 3'10"
wool, early 20th Cent.
This piece is typical of the primitive work done by
this Turkish tribal community.

118

CHAPTER VI

The fiercely independent nomads of the Caucasus fought back enemies for centuries to maintain control of their land. Their rugs reflect this spirit, and are valued for their robust geometric patterns and their well-balanced designs in vivid contrasting colors.

The peaks of the rugged Caucasus reach 17,000 feet and stretch seven hundred miles southeast from the Black Sea to the Caspian, creating a nearly impassable barrier between Europe and Asia. Across the Kura River valley to the south, the lesser Caucasus slope more gently, and grassy hills provide ample pasture for sheep. In this desolate mountain setting, the Caucasians wove some of the most sophisticated rugs of all times.

Although Caucasian weaving has been active since Homeric times, the earliest surviving pieces, known as the Dragon carpets, date only from the late seventeenth and eighteenth centuries. The majority of fine Caucasian rugs today belong to the nineteenth century. In the early nineteenth century, the Russians took over what are now the Soviet republics of Daghestan, Georgia, Armenia, and Azerbaijan—the heartland of Caucasian weaving. Through the Russian trade network of the late nineteenth century, Caucasian rugs reached Europe and enjoyed considerable popularity. European demand affected productivity and design, as many Karabaghs with distinctly French floral motifs appeared on the market (plate 83). Since the 1930s, production has continued in state factories and collectives; however, the more recent rugs lack the inspiration of the traditional homemade pieces. Russian and Pakistani artisans have tried to copy the earlier rugs, but without the unique wool of the mountain sheep and the rich natural dyes, their weaving cannot compare with the older pieces.

A final blow to the rug-making cultures came at the end of World War II. The obstinately autonomous peoples of the Caucasus had never accepted the doctrines of communism and had fled throughout Europe or volunteered to serve under the German Reich. At the end of the war, under the promise of Allied protection, the Caucasians returned, only to be massacred by the

Plate 56
KAZAK, 7'1" x 5'7"
wool, late 19th Cent.
The intentional mistake in the medallion and the rare
presence of a human figure add charm to this bold piece.

119

Soviets. Stalin deported many of the remaining tribes to Siberia. The great days of rug weaving in the Caucasus came to an end.

Unlike many modern Russian Caucasian rugs with cotton warp and weft, the traditional rugs of the Caucasus were almost always knotted on a wool warp and weft. The lean mountain sheep of the cold highlands provided lustrous fleece that looks and feels like silk. Today this glossy wool is one of the identifying characteristics of Caucasian rugs. The wool is usually left a natural brown or white for the warp, while the weft is often dyed pink or red, particularly in Kazaks. The top and bottom ends of the rugs frequently exhibit fringes braided into plaits. The sides are wrapped with white wool or cotton in Shirvans, blue wool in Kubas, and red or multicolored wool in other types.

The wool from the lower Caucasus, although still of excellent quality, does not match the high-altitude wool for warmth and soft thick pile. In the lowland regions of Kuba, Shirvan, and Baku, the weavers preferred the Turkish or Ghiordes knot and a short pile. In the mountainous areas of Kazak, Gendje, and Lesghi, weavers chose to leave the pile long and shaggy, and to use both the Turkish and Persian knot.

These wool rugs were traditionally dyed with natural dyes of the best quality (until the introduction of synthetic dyes in the second half of the nineteenth century). Used in lively juxtaposition, the bright colors of Caucasian rugs emphasize the forceful geometric designs. The rugs most often have several rows of borders framing a rectangular panel enriched with geometric designs. The artistry impresses us with the boldness of its scale, so evident in Kazak rugs, where angular medallions and large abstract shapes dominate the field (plates 17, 57). Often they contain the simplified, rectilinear versions of familiar Persian motifs such as rows of botehs or the herati pattern. Rows of geometric floral elements in diagonally alternating colors and stripes appear frequently, as in the Gendje Kazak (plate 99). Many of the patterns are reciprocal, for example, a Shirvan Kuba, where the distinction between figure and ground is ambiguous, creating a sophisticated optical game.

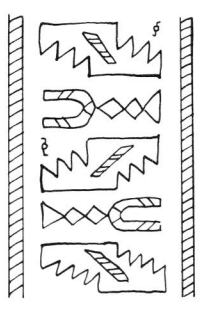

Oak leaf and Chalice

Plate 57
SEWAN KAZAK, 7' x 5'4"
wool, mid 19th Cent.
A truly outstanding example of this rare type of Kazak.
Exhibited, Museum of the Philadelphia Civic Center, 1978.
(Private Collection, New York)

The Caucasian weavers interjected many of the familiar figures and objects of their daily lives into their designs, punctuating the larger abstract forms with tiny human figures (plate 56), domestic animals including dogs, birds, camels (plate 29), and native flowers (plate 59). From the multitude of heavily stylized designs, the educated eye can also pick out boats, houses, graves, and combs. The meaning of these imaginative motifs is closely connected to tribal beliefs. The Christian Caucasians commonly used cruciferous forms, such as the eight-pointed Maltese Cross, and depicted churches; the Muslim weavers favored more abstract designs, particularly on prayer rugs. Despite the restriction on representing human figures in many sects of the Islamic faith, Caucasian rugs from traditionally Islamic tribes often figure shepherds, riders on horseback, and weavers. Many of the rugs woven as wedding gifts, or in celebration of feast days or funerals, contain related symbolism.

Certain symbols, such as the swastika, are universally held to be signs of good luck or a talisman against the evil eye; however, so many of the signs have been reworked, fused with other symbols, and repeated that it is difficult to ascertain their significance. As Caucasian rugs are products of a folk culture, they also reflect the village way of life and in many cases the personality of the weaver. The weaving was usually done in the home or tent by women who rarely, if ever, used cartoons. And, working from memory, they enjoyed improvising on traditional designs.

The size of Caucasian rugs suggests the semi-nomadic life of the weavers. The rugs were woven on portable, horizontal looms, which is why Caucasian rugs are usually three to five feet wide and three to seven feet long (with the exception of runners, which can reach twenty feet). The size of the nomadic looms was perfectly adapted to one of the most important objects in Islamic ritual, the prayer rug, measuring roughly five by three feet. These rugs often contain small amulets, latch-hook diamonds to avert the evil eye, or combs to symbolize cleanliness. Frequently, the weaver included dates woven into the corners (see Chapter II).

Today we think of two main types of Caucasian rugs: the Kazak, and the Kuba-Shirvan. The Kazak alone includes eleven different categories, and

Crab Flowers

Chichi border

Kufic border

Plate 58
SILEH KAZAK, 8' x 4'7"
wool, late 19th Cent.
This design is usually found in flatweave rugs called
verneh.
Exhibited, Museum of the Philadelphia Civic Center, 1978.

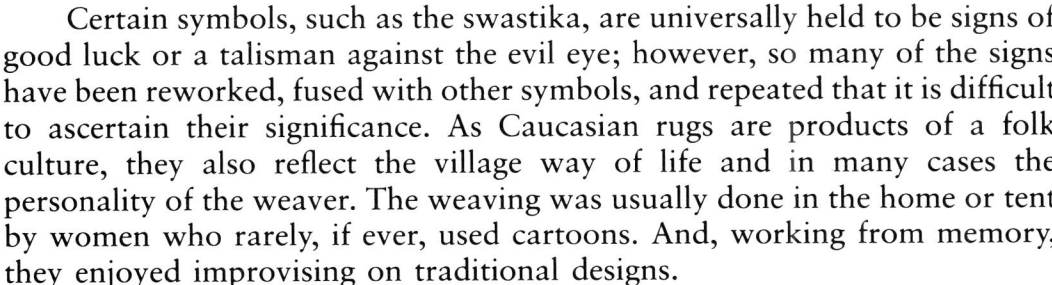

related to the Kazak are the Karabagh, Gendje, Talish, Moghan, and Lenkoran from the south and west. The second group runs from the east to the north, in which we can distinguish Shirvans (including Baku, Chila, Marasali, and Surahani), Kubas (Perpedil, Chichi, and Seichur), Daghestans, and Derbents. Attribution to these types is largely based on design, color, and structure; precise ethnic or geographic pinpointing is often a matter of intelligent guesswork.

Kazak
Region

The Kazak district was one of the most prolific rug-making areas of the last century. Stretching from Tiflis in Georgia to the more arid plains of Erivan in Armenia, and from Kars to the Moghan steppes, this region has held a mosaic of races and peoples. Christian Armenians, Moslem Kossacks, Kurds, and Turko-Tartars formed the principal weaving communities. There is considerable dispute among experts over the various subdivisions of Kazaks. Here we will merely distinguish some of the more commonly accepted types:

> Sewan Kazak
> Karatchoph Kazak
> Bordjalou Kazak
> Kazak with Silleh design
> Chondzoresk Kazak
> Chelaberd Kazak or Cloud Band Kazak
> Eagle Kazak
> Shield Kazak
> Kazak with Gendje design
> Kazak with Talish Center design

Most Kazaks have long pile, a fairly coarse weave, and wool with an exceptional sheen. They usually measure from three to five feet by five to eight feet.

Sewan
Kazak

The Sewan Kazak from the Lake Sewan area bears an elongated Maltese Cross framing the central design (plate 57). It is apparent why this type is often called the "Shield Kazak." This heraldic emblem, outlined in white, may hark back to ancient Turkoman double-arrowhead motifs. The source for this pattern is probably pre-Islamic. Some versions of the Sewan Kazak with a more rounded Maltese Cross are thought to represent water basins in a land

Plate 59
KAZAK, 7'8" x 4'5"
wool, late 19th Cent.
Persian influence is felt in the abstract gardens in
some of the lozenges.

where water is scarce. In our example, the unusual border features curled tendrils separated by stepped triangles.

Karachov

Closely related to the Sewan is the much sought-after type from the Karachov area. This design centers on a large octagon, perhaps related to the Turkoman gul, surrounded by projecting hooks which recall rams' horns. The latch-hooks found in many Caucasian rugs are often interpreted as symbols of happiness. Similar hooked devices can be seen in the corners of the field, along with small rectangular boxes. The main borders frame the composition with variants of a popular pattern called "serrated leaf and chalice," although the chalice may in fact be a floral device. Many collectors particularly value a deep emerald green as the most desirable field color.

Bordjalou

To the north of the Karachov district, vibrantly primal rugs, called Bordjalou, were produced (plate 60). The characteristic bright tomato-red field contains two concentric diamonds with hooked outlines, surrounded by a scattering of smaller ornaments suggestive of flowers, cradles, jugs, mirrors, and other symbolic objects. The wide border carries a reciprocal arrangement of the same hooked medallions halved into triangular shapes. Bordjalous usually run in fairly large sizes.

Gendje

Gendje rugs, from the town known today as Kirovabad, bear a close resemblance to Kazaks, but are lighter in color, with a preponderance of white and light blue. The edges are finished with multicolor overcasting rather than the traditional browns and reds. Instead of major medallions, Gendje weavers preferred small repeated geometric figures with diagonal color arrangements (plate 99).

Karabagh

The southeast district of Karabagh gave rise to rugs often indistinguishable from Kazaks, such as the rare "Sileh Kazak" (plage 58). The rug depicts the angular dragons more often seen in the type of flat-weave called Sileh. Dragons, believed to be Far Eastern in origin, are usually signs of happiness.

Eagle
Kazak

The "Eagle Kazak" comes from the village of Chelaberd in Karabagh (plate 17). The two-and-a-half flamboyant medallions may be derived from the earlier Dragon carpets. Other scholars interpret these bird-form medal-

Plate 60
BORDJALOU KAZAK, 7'6" x 5'7"
wool, late 19th Cent.
One of the most sought after of all Kazak rugs. This
piece is in mint condition.

lions as versions of the nineteenth-century Russian Imperial eagle. Still another school regards the medallion as a sunburst. Whatever the significance, the medallion, cut off by the border at the center, is suggestive of the Caucasian view of the field as a continuous and infinite space. The Eagle Kazak almost always has an ivory border with linked stars and a sawtooth secondary border.

Cloudband Kazak

From Chondzoresk, another well-known Karabagh design is often referred to as the Cloudband Kazak, after the four angular shapes arranged pinwheel-wise in the two or more bold medallions. The cloudband motif is believed to be Far Eastern in origin and bears the connotation of the celestial realm.

"Persian" Karabagh

Paralleling the more tribal Karabagh tradition, an earlier style of rug relates more closely to "Northwest Persian" design (plate 23). This is an outstanding early nineteenth century Karabagh clearly based on the Herati pattern. The rich floral latticework, intricately curvilinear in Persia, appears here as an angular and simplified translation. The deep saffron yellow found on this piece is a sign of age: it rarely occurs in later examples. The red and white reciprocal guard border adds an unmistakably Caucasian touch to the otherwise Persian concept. A deep reddish purple appears in many rugs from this same period. Russian rule of the area introduced European designs, witnessed by realistically drawn floral elements, such as the typical cluster of roses (plate 83).

Talish

To the southeast of the Karabagh district lie the Talish villages where a very rare form of long rug was woven (plate 65). The central field most commonly consists of a single deep Prussian blue strip, punctuated by a few small rosettes or totally devoid of decoration. The rich white border usually carries large rounded rosettes alternating with four small angular flower heads. Talishes feel velvety and their workmanship is finer than most Karabaghs or Kazaks. These particularly elegant Caucasian rugs have become quite rare.

Lenkoran

Lenkoran figures as one of the chief towns of the Talish district. Runners, approximately ten by four feet, have crab-like medallions and small octagons containing angular dragons depicted on a deep blue ground (plate 63). These motifs draw upon the Mongol tradition of the Tartar tribes who lived in the

Plate 61
SHIRVAN, 4'8" x 3'10"
wool, early 20th Cent.
An unusual design and coloration distinguish this piece.

Southern Caucasus from the fourteenth century onward. One of the most distinctive features of Lenkoran rugs is their thick, velvety wool, usually clipped to a medium length.

Traveling to the extreme southeast, we reach the region of Moghan, where the arid rocky steppe provided the last refuge for the nomadic way of life. The weavers of Moghan wove rugs mostly in runner sizes, keeping to light pastel shades. They employed patterns of repeated geometric floral and leaf devices, similar to many Kazaks and Talishes. Rows of octagonal patterns surrounded by hooked crosses were typical, as were polygons, executed with extreme precision in soft, lustrous wool. Few Moghans appear on the market today, particularly ones of the superb quality of which these weavers were capable.

The second major group of Caucasian rugs comes from the Kuba-Shirvan region along the eastern shore of the Caspian Sea. Often Kuba rugs are very difficult to tell from Shirvan rugs. In general, both of these types exhibit a finer weave and shorter pile than Kazaks. The designs tend to be less bold and more intricate, although large-scale patterns resembling Kazaks do occur. Many designs have been named after the village that originally produced them, but by the nineteenth century, these designs were widely copied, making identification by pattern alone unreliable. Often the only clues to origin are small structural details, such as the finish of the sides and ends, or the degree of depression in the warps observable on the back of the rug.

In general, Shirvan rugs may be distinguished by darker warp threads, white wool or cotton selvedges, and smooth backs with the warps all lying on the same level. The three-medallion design occurs frequently. Prayer rugs were a favorite, with the most popular coming from Marasali, known for its thin smooth pile and fine weave. A good example of this type features multicolor angular botehs on a midnight blue ground framed by the characteristic border of bird shapes facing alternately right and left (plate 67). These birds have been identified as parrots, symbols of good luck and deliverance from misfortune, following the legend that Genghis Khan was saved by his pet parrot.

The city of Baku, today a thriving oil center in Azerbaijan, was known for its rugs as early as the eighteenth century. In contrast to the robust texture of Kazaks, Baku rugs feel thin and pliable. While Kazaks display vigorous

Moghan

Kuba-Shirvan
Region

Shirvan

Baku

Plate 62
KHILA, 10'1" x 4'4"
wool, mid 19th Cent.
The soft colors and classic design of this rug
make it desirable with period furniture.
Plate 63
LENKORAN RUNNER, 10'5" x 3'4"
wool, late 19th Cent.
A typical design with a rare representation of a
pair of human figures.

colors, Bakus rely on subtle effects in a limited range of earth tones and turquoises. Particular to Baku rugs are intricate designs with variants of Kufic script along the borders and a complex play of interlocking lozenges (plate 94).

Khila

From Khila, a village in the Baku district, come some of the finest early examples of subtle design in rich pistachios, umbers, and lavenders (plate 62). In the second half of the nineteenth century, a rich variety of blues, from light turquoise to deep indigo, made their appearance in rugs, along with a characteristic polychrome striped border. A bold, almost three dimensional design of cruciform shapes and guls, reminiscent of Shirvans, was adapted to the Khila weave, which has a rough feel to the back. Like Marasali prayer rugs, many Khila rugs also depict rows of highly geometric botehs against a deep marine blue ground.

Surahani

Related to the earlier Khilas, Surahani rugs have a similar subdued chromatic range. These relatively rare rugs favor striking combinations of glowing earth tones set against pale fields.

Kuba

Immediately to the north of Shirvan lies the great rug-export center of Kuba. Rugs such as those in plates 66, 97, and 100 could be ascribed to either of the two districts in terms of design. Yet the structure of Kubas is often distinctive. The backs of Kubas are less smooth than Shirvans, because the alternate warps lie depressed. Kubas were especially famous for their beautiful blues; even the selvedges were of blue wool, and the ends often carried a few rows of sumak stitches in blue wool. Kuba rugs sometimes show four "star" medallions, known as "Lesghi Stars" after their repeated use in the rugs woven by the Lesghians to the north of Kuba (plate 97). These stars are variants of the Maltese Cross and are thought to refer to a divine celestial presence.

Seichur

Another medallion rug woven in the same silky pile and fine weave found in most Kubas originates from the neighborhood of Seichur (plate 64). The medallions, consisting of elaborate cross-like motifs, are often transformed into highly stylized dragons, or flowers. Another variety of Seichur rug adopted a European-style "cabbage rose" motif, rendered with a forceful Caucasian highlight of crimson and pink. These rugs are commonly framed by the "running dog" border (plate 82). The field pattern of another Seichur derives from the "Bidjov" design, named after a village in the Shirvan area.

Plate 64
SEICHUR, 5'10" x 3'7"
wool, late 19th Cent.
A delightful design with swans and Lesghi medallions.

South of Seichur, close to the Caspian Sea, the weavers of Perepedil wove some of the most distinctive rugs; easily recognizable by a repeated design of ram horns known as "wurma" etched in white against a deep blue indigo field complemented by borders and minor designs in earth tones. Frequently the border bears a star design or a vase and chalice motif and on occasion a kufic pattern. (plate 20, 96)

Perepedil

It is wide border of the Chichi rug—with it alternating quadrefoil rosette and diagonal ban motif—which allows collectors to identify it at once. Made in a village to the southwest of Perpedil in the Kuba district, these finely woven, low pile rugs with a field of compact stepped polygons, are highly sought after by Caucasian rug connoisseurs. (plate 18)

Chichi

Along the extreme northern edge of the Caucasus runs the Daghestan ("the land of mountains") with its capital of Derbent. This region, most celebrated for its precisely woven prayer rugs, continues to produce a large quantity of rugs of various types. The Lesghian tribes of these mountains made shaggy, tightly woven rugs with a firm, compact feel. Exquisite white ground prayer rugs with honeycomb lattice flower head patterns are excellent examples of the fine workmanship of Daghestan.

Daghestan

Caucasian rug districts produced various flat-weave tapestries that go by the names of palas, kilim, sumak, verneh, and Sileh (see Chapter II, "Flat-weaves"). These were intended mostly for home use as hangings, coverlets, carriage covers, and bags. Verneh and Sileh are highly characteristic types, the former usually divided into red, blue, and green rectangular compartments containing fanciful animals, and the latter known for its angular S-shaped dragons covered with a multitude of small scales. The numerous types of kilims include large (up to ten by six feet) tapestries in the slit-weave technique, usually carrying rows of hooked X shapes or polygons in red, white, blue, and green.

Flat-weave

If the name Sumak is any indication of probable origin, this technique may have evolved in the Caucasus from the town of Shemaka. Soumaks were made all along the Caspian in a variety of patterns including medallions and overall repeats (plates 33, 34). Now that these pieces are becoming appreciated by collectors, some excellent new scholarship, such as the studies by Anthony Landreau and W. R. Pickering, has thrown light on the origins and fascinating varieties of flat-weaves.

Wurmas

Plate 65
TALISH RUNNER, 11′2″ x 3′10″
wool, late 19th Cent.
One of the rarest and most interesting designs of the Caucasian area. This is a typical example in which the plain blue center contrasts with the colorful border.
Plate 66
KUBA KARABAGH RUNNER, 10′8″ x 3′8″
wool, early 20th Cent.
A Persian influenced design with a "Kufic" border.

Scholarship   The study of Caucasian rugs is complex and relatively recent. One of the major problems in grouping Caucasian rugs was, until the mid-sixties, the lack of a single, consistent terminology. Some names indicate the tribe of weavers, some refer to locality, while others are purely fictional. The term "Kabistan," for example, used indiscriminately in the trade for Kubas and Shirvans, may be a misreading of Ghabristan, meaning "graveyard." The association apparently arose from the fact that many prayer rugs coming from this region were used for devotional purposes in graveyards, or as part of the funeral paraphernalia. Serious scholarship has cleared up many of these misnomers, with Schurmann's pioneering study, *Caucasian Rugs*, leading the way in 1964.

Although Caucasian rugs have been collected for over a hundred years, they were first exhibited in a major museum show in 1961 in Hamburg, Germany, followed by similar exhibits in Frankfort in 1962, and in Washington, D.C. in 1967. More recently, the Museum of Philadelphia Civic Center, *The Heritage of the East*, featured an important selection of Caucasian rugs, including many of the rare pieces shown in this volume. However, the vast majority of fine Caucasian rugs are still in the Soviet Union and many remain in the hands of private collectors. It is not surprising that the appeal of the Caucasian rug has been understood by so few up to now, as it requires a particular sensibility to a culture that forged a bold art form of its own. This distinctive nomadic craft is no longer alive, which has made fine Caucasian rugs so valuable today.

Plate 67
MARASALI PRAYER, 4'11" x 3'4"
wool, late 19th Cent.
An intricate, highly colored design with an outstanding "dragon" border, typical of this tribe's output.

CHAPTER VII

The rugs of these once feared Turkomans form the most easily recognizable group, with their predominantly red tones and severe geometric grids carrying octagonal and diamond-shaped tribal insignia called "guls." These familiar repeated motifs reflect the great age of this nomadic weaving tradition, which may have created the oldest surviving rug, the Pazyryk Carpet (see Chapter II).

TURKOMAN RUGS

Turkestan, the land of the Turkomans, is a rugged territory of arid steppe and desert punctuated by oases. It stretches eight hundred miles east of the Caspian Sea to the Hindu Kush and Pamir Mountains, and spans four hundred miles from the Aral Sea in the north to the Kopet Dagh Mountains of Iran in the south. The few cities—Khiva, Merv, Bokhara, Samarkand— occupy strategic oases and serve as market centers for the region. Although several cities have given their names to rugs, few were actually woven in these places. Furthermore, the cities are inaccurate guides to tribal attribution, since they changed hands frequently during the stormy nineteenth century.

The khanates (principalities) of Khiva and Bokhara predominated until the 1860s. Their rivalry enlisted the various Turkoman tribes as mercenaries, exploiting their traditional struggle for the richest grazing grounds. The Salor and Saryk tribes were early victims of this war. They ceased to exist as tribal entities by the time the Tekke emerged as victors. These tribal splintering and fusions further complicate attribution of their rugs.

The ancient independent nomadic life-style of the Turkomans was disrupted by Russian Imperial expansion into Transcaspia (the first scholarly study of Turkoman rugs was done by General Bogoliouboff, the Russian military governor of the Transcaspian Provinces in 1908). The Russian takeover in the 1880s brought, along with an increasing demand for tribal weavings, the inevitable synthetic dyes, gradual commercialization, and eventual mass production. This led in most cases to a decline: designs became simplified, guls more compressed, borders less elaborate, and colors harsher. However, until these Turkoman tribes were incorporated into several Soviet

Plate 68
HATCHLI PRAYER, 4'10" x 3'9"
wool, early 20th Cent.
Turkoman rugs with intricate designs and economy of
color are much sought after by collectors.

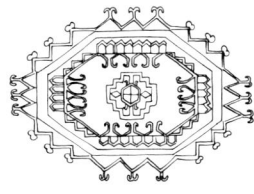

Salor gul

Republics in the 1920s, the weavers in these territories continued to produce outstanding examples of traditional art.

The various tribes had been known for centuries as the Salor, Saryk, Tekke, and Yomud, nomadic wanderers who, in their generally westward movements, intermarried with Indo-Persian natives and adopted Islam. The Turkoman tribes were primarily herders of sheep, goats, and camels. Although portions of the tribes farmed, forming the settled group called "chomur," the majority belonged to the ruling "chovra," or migratory element. The latter were fearless riders who indulged in an occasional raid, taking captives and holding them for ransom. The women performed the household work, including rug weaving, although the men were in charge of dyeing the wool. As nomads valued these rugs highly, the prosperity of a family was often measured by the number of women engaged in making them.

The majority of nineteenth-century rugs were made for home use in the "kibitka" (tents). Edmond O'Donovan, a traveler in Merv in 1880, described the setting of these mostly small rugs:

Saryk gul

"The furniture of these tents (the dome-shaped wicker-hut, with its covering of reed mats and felt) is very simple. The fire occupies the middle of the apartment, immediately under the central opening in the dome. The half of the floor remote from the entrance is covered with a ketche, or felt carpet, nearly an inch in thickness. On this are laid, here and there, Turkoman carpets, six or seven feet long by four to five in breadth, on which the inhabitants sit by day and sleep by night . . .
Round the walls hang large flat camel-bags, six feet by four, one side being entirely composed of the rich carpetwork in which the Turkoman women excel. Ordinarily, all the household goods are packed in these bags, for transit from place to place on the back of camels."

The most common formats woven on small portable looms were:
Torba, long and narrow storage bag, usual size 14–20 by 36–44 inches.
Juval, larger storage bag also used for bedding, 30–48 by 42–68 inches.

Plate 69
TEKKE, 10'1" x 7'
wool, late 19th Cent.
An extremely fine example. The flatweave skirts have an
unusual design distinguishing this from more typical pieces.

Khordjin, saddlebag, 16–24 by 20–28 inches.

Tang, external tent band, very long strip 6–14 inches wide, up to 40 feet long.

Osmolduk, five-sided rug used as animal trapping for wedding processions, 20–34 by 30–48 inches.

Engsi (pardah), door hanging or prayer rug, usually in hatchli (cruciform) design, 48–60 by 60–84 inches.

Qalin, floor covering, "main carpet," up to 5–7 by 11–12 feet.

Most of these formats were produced in flat-woven as well as knotted techniques. The knotting, most often Senneh (although some tribes such as the Yomud prefer the Turkish knot), is fine to very fine. Occasionally one may find a piece in the Senneh knot with a few rows of Turkish knots near the edge. A long kilim strip marks the top and bottom ends. Wool and sometimes small amounts of silk or cotton are used. The warp and weft often contain an admixture of goat hair. The sides are frequently overcast with brown goat hair.

The basic Turkoman color is madder red, in any of an endless variety of shades from liver, oxblood, and brick red, to violet, brown, plum, chocolate, mahogany, and chestnut. A bright synthetic carmine known as "Russian red" was introduced in the late nineteenth century and used at first in limited amounts. Indigo served for blue, mostly in its darkest blue-black (surmey) shade, or as a lovely light blue, found especially in earlier pieces. The limited use of yellow, green, and ivory highlights, and black or dark brown outlines creates subtle effects that alleviate color monotony.

The hatchli design seen in door hangings consists of a cruciform division of the field into four rectangular panels, usually carrying horizontal rows of Y-shaped motifs variously identified as shrubs or rams' horns. Occasionally, a small prayer arch, or a series of them, may be included at one end of the field, indicating that this door hanging may have doubled as a prayer rug.

The most common Turkoman design employs a restricted vocabulary: a grid with octagonal or diamond-shaped major guls at the intersections, and other geometric devices known as minor guls in the spaces between. Originally, each tribe featured one or more highly specific insignia, or gul;

Yomud Ertmen gul

Yomud Dyrnak gul

Plate 70
YOMUD, 11'2" x 7'3"
wool, late 19th Cent.
The long kilim skirts of this outstanding piece
indicate the age and high standards of craftsmanship.

these were displayed only on the large "main carpets." When a tribe, such as the Salor, suffered defeat and disintegrated, the victorious group, such as the Tekke, appropriated the emblems of the vanquished. Gradually various tribes borrowed and adapted famous guls, often simplifying them in the process.

The following classification by tribe applies mostly to the Turkoman rugs of the nineteenth century.

MAJOR TRIBES

Salor

The Salor tribe, mentioned by Arab geographers as early as the eleventh century, was on the wane by the nineteenth century, when it suffered defeat at the hands of the Saryk and Tekke. Up to that time, the Salor lived around Merv, and their distinctive gul is called the Merv or "Mar" gul, identifiable by the small turret-like projections around its perimeter. Precision of drawing and finely articulated multiple narrow borders are characteristic of the best Salor rugs.

Saryk

The Saryk tribe, a close relative of the Salor, was scattered shortly after the downfall of the Salor. Many of the tribe fled to Afghanistan, where they continued to make rugs in the Saryk manner. These are some of the most somber of the Turkoman rugs, the older Saryks being distinguished by a brown-purple tone.

Tekke

Since the Tekke emerged as the dominant tribe in the nineteenth century, their rugs are the best known, having been exported to the West after the Russian conquest. Often the dividing line between Salor, Saryk, and Tekke is indistinct, because the former two tribes were partially absorbed by their conquerors. The Akhal Tekke lived around Ashkabad (present-day capital of the Turkmen Soviet Socialist Republic), while other groups of Tekke lived to the east. The characteristic Tekke gul may be seen in a more rounded form in the earlier rugs. Unlike the several lesser border stripes in the Saryk and Salor rugs, Tekkes have a major border usually repeating a radiating "sunburst" rosette. A warm brick red is the usual favorite ground color. The Tekke made large numbers of engsi in the hatchli design (plate 68). Here, the ground color is a mellow abrashed medium red, and the main border of shrubs with serrated blue and white leaves carries over into the top panel of the skirt. The bottom panel contains a lattice of eight-pointed flower heads on a natural brown ground. The light blue and the generous, uncrowded spacing of the shrubs in the field are early features in this prayer rug.

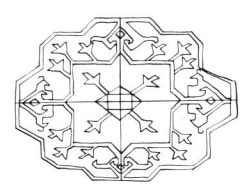

Tekke guls

Yomud

The widely scattered Yomud tribe originally occupied western Turkestan, especially around Khiva and near the Caspian Sea. Because of the many subgroups, such as the Goklan, Jafarbai, and Ogurdjali, there is great

Plate 71
BESHIR BOKHARA, 5'2" x 3'2"
wool, early 20th Cent.
Prayer rugs of the Beshir tribe are extremely rare, and this is a fine example of the type.

variation in characteristics, and a number of different guls—dyrnak, ertmen, kepse—are used equally. Among the Yomud, the Turkish knot is more prevalent than the Persian knot, and the knotting is less fine than in other Turkoman groups, save for that of the Ersari. They favor liverish red, plum, light blue, yellow, and apricot. A "main carpet" features the dyrnak gul (plate 70). The light blue-green and apricot are effectively highlighted. The variation in the small rectangular panels between the octagons of the main border indicates age (later pieces show a more uniform treatment). The end panels contain handsome trees with multicolor serrated leaves bearing unique flower heads. The long kilim strips in red with narrow blue stripes complete the impression of considerable age conveyed by this harmonious rug. Later Yomuds, outstanding for fine and tight weave, typify rugs custom-made for the European luxury market. The larger sizes elaborate borders, and the colors cater to Western needs and tastes. The dark plum fields are enlivened by the brilliant cochineal red used in the guls.

The Chodor tribe was at one time identified with a subgroup of the Yomud. The two tribes share some guls, such as the ertmen, but Chodor rugs may be told by their deep chocolate ground color.

The Ersari, one of the oldest Turkoman groups on record, migrated in the seventeenth century from the Manguishlak district near the Caspian to the Bokhara region and down to Afghanistan. The subdivisions include the Chub-bash, the Beshire, and some Afghan tribes.

Some of the oldest surviving examples of Turkoman rugs belong to Ersari types (plate 21). This remarkable piece is unusual in all aspects: length, design and coloration. Rows of diamond-shaped guls with triangles of coral, yellow and jade green highlights enliven the predominately coral field. The field itself is further enhanced by a delicate white grid pattern and is flanked on either side with a simple single border of rosettes. In addition to the other features, the long rust-colored kilim skirt indicates considerable age. Ersari rugs have the lightest and brightest colors of the Turkoman rugs, most frequently a cherry red ground, with yellow, green, and light blue. Goat hair often constitutes at least a portion of the warp and weft. Ersari juval show the tribal preference for bright colors. The rare Ersari (Beshire) prayer rugs are much sought by collectors.

Yomud Kepse gul

Chodor

Ersari

Ersari gul

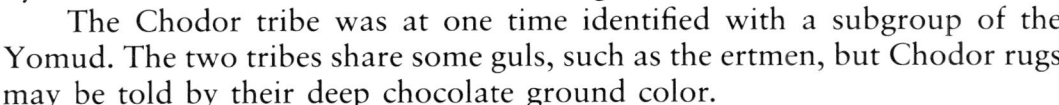

Plate 72
BELOUCH, 6′10″ x 3′4″
wool, early 20th Cent.
The color and design of this rug are typical of this
nomadic tribe at the turn of the century.

Baluchi

Afghan gul

Baluchi rugs are produced by a number of tribes at various locations, mostly in the Khorasan province of Iran, Afghanistan, and Pakistan. Although many Persian and even Caucasian features occur in Baluchi rugs, as a group they are most closely affiliated to the Turkoman. Their rugs fall into smaller formats and contain much camel and goat hair in addition to wool. The color scheme is related to the Turkoman, with madder reds, indigo, and brown predominant, and a sparing use of white for borders and highlights. The Tree of Life design was very popular among the Baluchi, often worked on a camel ground. Their small prayer rugs frequently use this motif as well. Flat-woven utility bags exemplify the kind of finely worked nomadic artifact that has become collectible recently. Good Baluchi rugs are among the last authentic tribal pieces still generally available on the market for the knowing collector (plate 72, 73).

Scholarship

There is probably more disagreement on Turkoman nomenclature than on any other type of rug. A. A. Bugoliouboff's two-volume *Tapisseries de l'Asie Central* written in 1880, is a key work. More recent studies have been provided by Amos Thatcher, Ulrich Schurman, S. Azadi, and V. G. Moshkova.

Turkoman rugs are just beginning to be truly appreciated by collectors. Two major exhibitions in recent years, *Ancient Art of the Asian Steppes and Highlands* at the Los Angeles County Museum of Art in 1978, and *Turkoman Rugs from the Ashkhabad Museum* in Paris at the Musée de l'Homme in 1979, have made this art form available to the public. There is also a growing appreciation for these rugs on the part of designers who now can purchase relatively inexpensive imitations of the finer, older pieces. As stated in chapter I, "Investment," it has become clear from the sale of Turkoman bagfaces that these pieces are rapidly becoming a prime target for the investment market. Today's output of quality workmanship is extremely small, and has further diminished with the volatile political situations in these regions.

Plate 73
BELOUCH, 5'10" x 3'10"
wool, c. 1950
This is a typical example of the current products of
the Belouch tribe.

CHAPTER VIII

The Persian love of gardens was shared by the Moguls during India's short-lived flowering of rug weaving, which will be dealt with briefly here. The emperor Babur was famous for the gardens he laid out, often supervising the work himself, as witnessed by contemporary miniature paintings. The rugs reflected this fascination with horticulture by presenting lifelike images of flora and fauna not seen in any other group of weavings. Trees, flowers, and wildlife are shown in extremely faithful renderings, so that the species may be identified. Extraordinarily fine knotting made this precision possible. The colors of these rugs in general were softer and lighter than their Persian counterparts, favoring a rich carmine pink. Prayer rugs in the millefleur style, hunting carpets, and fantastic animal-vegetable compositions were among the most typical products of the Mogul era. After the Moguls were overthrown in 1738, rugs continued to be made in India, but they were of an inferior quality. The arrival of the British resulted in the migration of some of the finest rugs to England.

Although the inspiration of early Indian rug designs was largely Persian, the two styles may be told apart by a closer look. In Indian rugs, natural forms are carefully and realistically depicted, whereas Persian artistry usually transforms these motifs into highly stylized designs. The rug art of India favors asymmetrical composition with great articulation of individual forms, while Persians tend toward symmetrical designs and more subtle orchestration of them.

The oldest weaving centers were concentrated in the northwest of India, near Kashmir, and the northern parts of present-day Afghanistan and Pakistan. Chief among the centers were Lahore, Fatpur, and Agra, where production continued into the nineteenth century. In the nineteenth century, India began to export large numbers of rugs of generally inferior quality that were mostly reproductions of Persian designs in cotton. (As these have little investment value, we will not dwell on them here.) A few traditional centers, such as Agra, near Kashmir, still produced high-quality rugs (plate 75). At

Plate 74
ZIEGLER MAHAL, 14'1" x 9'11"
wool, late 19th Cent.
The Ziegler firm commissioned many rugs for their
European clients. This piece contains a "gul hinani" design.

this time, the reputation of Indian rugs was also severely damaged by the introduction of commercial products made by prison labor in towns such as Bangalore and Mirzapur. These large, heavy pieces, woven mostly of cotton, were coarse and of such low grade that at one time they were not allowed into the United States.

Other centers of more recent production are Srinagar and Amritsar, where the finer nineteenth-century examples originated. Oriental Carpet Manufacturers and C. M. Hadow and Company stimulated the rug industry by acquiring contracts, organizing the workshops, training weavers, and establishing quality controls for rug production.

Active rug centers are now at Allahabad, Mirzapur, Madras, and Vellore. These places make a great many cotton rugs, as well as the more indigenous dhurries, large flat-weaves with bold geometric designs and brilliant colors. A fine early-twentieth-century example of a dhurrie was made of silk with metallic threads (plate 32). These large and openly spacious flat-weaves have become increasingly popular in contemporary interior design, and are favored for floor coverings in summer houses.

Exhibitions

Many of the fine Indian rugs brought to England by the British can be seen in various private collections there. In the United States, the Metropolitan Museum of Art in New York houses a major collection with frequent exhibitions of the best pieces in the Islamic Wing of the museum. Period Indian rugs appear very rarely on the market. When they are sold, prices can equal Persian rugs of the same period and condition; one such example of a Mogul rug brought $66,600 at a Monte-Carlo sale in 1978.

Today, excellent merchandising and inexpensive labor have made India number one in quantity of rugs produced. And, after a period of slack and poor-quality production, a revival in the industry is beginning to lead to better quality control. While these rugs are readily available on the market, their value is primarily decorative.

Plate 75
AGRA, 17'7" x 12'2"
wool, early 20th Cent.
A large piece produced in India's primary rug center.

CHAPTER IX

The rugs of China and East Turkestan form a unique group among Oriental rugs. They are readily distinguishable by designs familiar to Western eyes through Chinese porcelains and paintings. Chinese designs, arranged symmetrically along a grid, are striking in their simplicity and contrasting color schemes such as blue and white. An elaborate and explicit vocabulary of symbols depicted with meticulous care adds a fascinating dimension of meaning to the controlled designs. Most of these motifs pre-date the art of rug-making in China; thirteenth-century Chinese paintings depict Mongol rather than Chinese rugs, and few Chinese rugs can be dated with any certainty to as early as the Ming dynasty in the seventeenth century.

China originally held eighteen provinces, and stretched from the Great Wall to Outer Mongolia. Most rugs were woven in northern China, although some were produced in the south. The four northern provinces particularly active in the weaving industry were Ninghsia, Suiyuan, Chadhar, and Jehol. Important centers also developed along the two great rivers of China, the main arteries of communication: Lanchow, Paotua, Kalgan, Jehol, and Shanhaikuan on the Hang Ho River; and Hankow, Nanking, and Shanghai on the Yangtze Kiang River.

Rugs probably entered China rather late through an area known as Chinese Turkestan, located in the eastern section of the great plateau which has been under Chinese jurisdiction for over a thousand years. It is composed of a mixed ethnic group of people united by a common language, known as Jagatai Turkish. These semi-nomadic groups settled in oasis towns, the best known of which are Kashgar, Khotan, and Yarkand (plate 81).

We know from rug fragments discovered by A. LeCoq and Sir Aurel Stein that East Turkestan has made rugs since the third century. More recent rugs made in the Tarim Basin in the northern province of Sinkiang rarely appear on the market. They come from the oasis cities of Samarkand, Yarkand, Kashgar, and Khotan, although Bidder claims most were produced at Khotan. The palette of these rugs is lighter than in Chinese rugs, favoring

CHINESE RUGS

East
Turkestan

Plate 76
PEKING CHINESE, 10' x 8'
wool, late 19th Cent.
The quiet design and subtle colors make the Peking rugs
among the most desirable of the Chinese output.

red, yellow, and blue. The Turkestan weavers often employ silk or metallic threads, and these rugs evince as much Persian influence as Chinese. The most common design is the disk medallion, as seen in this outstanding Yarkand rug (plate 81). Here the abrashed deep salmon ground carries a blue central medallion with four quarter medallions occupying the corners. Horizontal bands of light blue and a Chinese-flavored panel of chevrons at each end complete the design. The pomegranate and vase, the boxed chrysanthemum gul, and overall patterns such as the herati often occur in East Turkestan rugs. Occasionally one finds multiple prayer rugs (saph) emulating a popular Turkoman prayer-rug type.

DATING

The everpresent tendency to copy older styles was carried to an extreme in China, and has complicated precise dating of Chinese rugs. Scholars—H. A. Lorentz, David Wang, and Murray Eiland, among others—have traced the development of these rugs largely through the use of certain colors and patterns, and technical features. While there are distinct styles within each region, they have not yet been sufficiently studied for treatment of the rugs according to region. For the moment, it makes more sense to treat them by period.

Ming Dynasty

The few extant rugs from the seventeenth century Ming dynasty show finely drawn, elaborate dragon and phoenix designs, such as the rug at the Metropolitan Museum of Art called the Ming rug, or referred to simply as the "Chinese Fragment." Typical of this period are warm red-browns and yellows complementing dark indigos, and borders forming a very narrow frame. A fine piece reflecting the ancient style has a restricted palette of dark brown floral sprigs twisting on a field of deep gold, surrounded by an inner strip of light blue and an outer border of traditional swastikas in an endless chain.

Ch'ien Lung Period

The eighteenth century, known as the Ch'ien Lung period, marked the appearance of several new colors, such as light blue, peach, and fawn, along with delicately drawn floral elements, peony borders, and medallions. Overall diaper and fret patterns were also popular around this time. In medallion designs, four medallions may appear in the corners of the rug, in addition to the single central medallion. In general, the Ch'ien Lung period may be

Plate 77
CHINESE, 6'1" x 3'
silk, c. 1940
China has continued to produce rugs of quality throughout the 20th Century; this is one of a pair.

158

considered the Renaissance of Chinese rug weaving. Many of the eighteenth-century characteristics described above also occur in rugs woven in the nineteenth century (plate 76).

By the nineteenth century, in addition to madder reds and golds ranging from carmine to amber, a peach blush tint was achieved by dyeing first with yellow, then with madder. At the same time, quieter and more sparsely decorated rugs, with open fields and a few scattered floral ornaments around central medallions, were also made. These rugs prove that noble and even austere compositions continued to be created throughout the nineteenth century.

By the second half of the nineteenth century (after 1856), China became fully open to Western trade. New workshops sprang up in Peking, Tientsin, and Ninghsia. In trade, only two basic distinctions were made in rugs: Ninghsia denoted any piece of quality, while any coarse piece was called Peking. Around the turn of the century, the introduction of aniline dyes led to garish, harsh colors in greens, pinks, and golds. Traditional designs of dragons and florals ballooned in size to occupy the whole rug. The average size of rugs increased also, to accommodate large Western houses, and Western demand for "bedroom sets"—two runners and a large carpet—elicited much production in this format.

Synthetic dyes slowly improved, as did the texture and weave of the rugs themselves. Deep purple, lilac, jade, and wine red grounds supported gracefully supple flower and leaf sprays and satisfied the Art Deco taste.

Apart from the traditional palace and temple floor coverings, the Chinese often preferred scatter rugs for furniture coverings and beddings. Special formats included scalloped seat covers and saddle rugs, as well as round rugs. An example of a wall hanging depicts a pair of handsome peacocks at each end, done in blues with red highlights on an ivory ground (plate 77). A long, narrow runner features sparse floral clusters on a dark blue field surrounded by a floral meander pattern on a lighter blue border (plate 79). Room-size rugs were mostly aimed at the Western markets.

Plate 78
CHINESE, 7' 1" x 4'
wool, early 20th Cent.
A very unusual design, perhaps intended for temple use.

160

Techniques/
Materials

Technically, Chinese rugs do not compete with the fine weave and suppleness of Persian and Turkoman rugs. They are usually quite coarsely knotted with the Senneh knot; however, this seems ideally suited to the themes of spacious fields scattered with ornamental motifs. The coarseness of the weave is sometimes augmented by incising or embossing the surface to produce sharper outlines and a sculpted effect. Earlier rugs were even coarser and shorter napped. To suit Western tastes, modern rugs have less closely clipped naps, leaving the pile at least half an inch or longer. This feature contributes to the long wear of Chinese rugs.

Sheep's wool, originally not produced in China proper in any quantity, came in abundance from Mongolia through trade with the nomads. Tibet provided wool of the best quality, along with goat and yak hair. Camel wool was mostly reserved for the beautiful beige and ivory tones in Chinese rugs. Rugs woven for special occasions called for silk and metallic threads. The warp of Chinese rugs is almost invariably cotton.

SYMBOLS

Unlike most other types of Oriental rugs, Chinese rugs convey quite specific messages with their decorative symbols. These often ancient conventions were readily legible to an educated audience within the cultural framework that produced them, but they need interpretation for the Western viewer. All aspects of Chinese tradition—Taoist, Confucian, and Buddhist—appear and overlap in these symbols. It must be noted that the meanings described here are simplifications of profound philosophical beliefs and are subject to varied interpretations.

Foremost of an ancient group of simple geometric symbols is the swastika, or hooked cross. It symbolizes "good luck" if used singly, and "ten-thousandfold happiness" if seen in an endless diaper pattern or fretwork border. The "pearl" border and the "T" and "key" patterns all originated in equally ancient times, and appear on the earliest Chinese bronze ceremonial objects.

Another basic symbol of great antiquity, the "yin-yang," represents the interlocking, inseparable duality of female and male, dark and light, cold and heat. Sometimes the yin-yang forms the center of a medallion surrounded by

Plate 79
CHINESE RUNNER, 9'8" x 2'
wool, c. 1930
The Chinese made rugs in great numbers in the 1920's
primarily for export to Europe and America, where they were popular in Art Deco interiors.
Plate 80
CHINESE COLUMN RUG, 7'10" x 2'8"
wool, late 19th Cent.
These rugs were made to surround columns in temples
and palaces.

162

the Eight Trigrams (pa-kua). There are triple combinations of broken and unbroken lines that form sub-units of the hexagrams in the *I-Ching*, and different arrangements have different meanings: heaven, wind, earth, fire, water, mountain, thunder, clouds. The Chinese character "shou" (long life) often appears in a somewhat stylized version in medallions. Another word, "fu" (luck) explains the presence of all those bats in Chinese rugs: the word for bat is also "fu."

The elements of nature—water, cloud, mountain, fire—that play such an important role in the symbology of the *I-Ching* frequently appear in conventionalized form. Calm water, denoted by semicircles, and rough water, with squarish or triangular shapes, are often combined with concentric scalloped triangles that signify mountain and rock. Occasionally, small dots or cloud shapes suggest sea foam. Lightning and fire similarly take on stylized abbreviations.

The rich storehouse of mythical creatures includes the dragon, who plays a totally different role from his gruesome and repulsive Western counterpart. In Chinese art, the dragon symbolizes the supreme majesty of nature, its driving energy. Translated into the human sphere, the five-clawed dragon stands for the emperor. A splendid example of a dragon carpet presents a lavishly elaborate treatment of this favorite theme, in the traditional austere color scheme of dark and light blue with ivory and auburn highlights on a soft ground of old gold (plate 7). Ringed by an elegant tracery of arabesque branches and blossoms, the central dragon occupies its medallion accompanied by lightning, clouds, and the pearl. The pearl is one of eight precious things symbolizing luck; it is also a charm against fire and flood. The central dragon's four companions occupy the corners of the field that is surrounded by multiple floral borders.

The phoenix (feng-huang), typically seen as a hybrid pheasant, peacock, and crane, usually represents the empress. Unicorns (ch'i lin) combine the head of a dragon, the body of a stag, the tail of an ox, and the hooves of a horse. Flying through the sky with flames rising from its shoulders, the unicorn lives a thousand years and appears at the birth of sages. Fu-dogs (shitzu) resemble lions, and are the reputed watchdog guardians of Buddhist holy places.

Plate 81
YARKAND, 10' x 4'
wool, late 19th Cent.
Samarkand and Yarkand, on the borders of China, produced
many rugs in fine wools with Chinese design motifs.
(Courtesy of Eskenazi, Milan)

Animals seen in Chinese rugs may be the ones assigned to the hours of the day. Animals also denote the twelve sectors of the Chinese zodiac: horse, dog, bullock, monkey, serpent, dragon, rabbit, rat, tiger, hare, fowl, and boar. Storks and cranes symbolize old age and longevity, horses nobility, and fishes abundance. Butterflies are a rebus for long life.

The supreme floral symbol, the lotus, rising from muddy waters, conveys the purity of the divine. The chrysanthemum and peony, together with the narcissus, emblems of constancy and riches, round out the four flowers that stand for the seasons. The peach is the most auspicious fruit, followed in popularity by the pomegranate, paragon of fertility. The Chinese artists also liked the citron because of the resemblance of its rinds to the hands of a reposing Buddha.

At times, pictorial rugs carry entire groups of symbols, such as the Buddhist Eight Emblems: wheel of the law, conch shell, state umbrella, canopy, lotus, covered vase, pair of fishes, endless knot. Or they may use the eight symbols of Taoism: fan, sword, staff and gourd, castanets, basket of flowers, flute, bamboo, and lotus pod.

It follows that such a rich array of symbolic ornament served ceremonial and ritual functions, as in the case of temple rugs. The most characteristic of these is the column or pillar rug that was wrapped around pillars so that its sides met. A very unusual representative of this group shows a mythological creature, with its head at one end and its backbone running down the middle of the rug (plate 80). The other end of the rug contains a conventional wave-foam-rock configuration. Another temple rug depicts five dragons on a purple field scattered with clouds and flaming pearls (plate 78). A multicolored mountain and cloud pattern composes the border.

Scholarship/
Exhibitions

Recent publications, such as Murray Eiland's *Oriental and Exotic Rugs*, and *The David Te Chin Wang Collection* are gradually casting light on the provenance and dating of Chinese rugs. Chinese rugs are also benefiting from a new wave of interest in the Far Eastern Oriental art market. Along with Far Eastern antique ceramics, paintings, and sculptures, according to an August 1979 issue of *Business Week*, Chinese rugs are becoming heavily in demand as reflected in current auction prices. In 1979, following an extraordinary museum exhibition in Zurich in 1978, the David Te Chin Wang collection was auctioned off and attained some the highest prices ever paid for Chinese rugs. And a Ming dynasty saddle rug auctioned at Sotheby's in London in 1978 went for a record price. This indicates an upward trend in fine Chinese rugs, whose quiet elegance is appreciated by contemporary designers.

Plate 82
SEICHUR, 4′1″ x 2′11″
wool, early 20th Cent.
Seichur was known for its rugs with rose motifs, made
for the European market.

CHAPTER X

Virtually every country throughout Europe has produced rugs, but the main countries were France, England, Spain, Germany, Scandinavia, Belgium, Poland, Greece, and Portugal. Here we will discuss only those countries that generated important trends and designs and produced rugs in large quantities.

By the twelfth century, the Moors had established an important and influential rug industry on the Iberian Peninsula which continued to flourish under the Christian domination. The main centers of rug production were at Chinchilla, Leturi, Alcaraz, and Mudejar. The fusion of Moorish and Western design created a style called "Mudejar" which later influenced Spain's famous heraldic rugs. By the sixteenth century, Cuenca had become a prosperous center, producing rugs inspired by contemporary Turkish designs woven in the Turkish knot. In the mid-eighteenth century, a royal factory was established in Madrid that manufactured rugs to rival the Savonnerie industry. The oriental designs slowly died out, and by the nineteenth century, rugs were produced in the Aubusson style, although in lighter colors than in the French models.

The famous exhibition in Madrid in 1933 coincided with the end of the glorious Spanish weaving tradition. The output of the royal looms, such as those at Madrid, diminished after their civil war. Today, primarily decorative pieces in the rustic Alpujarra style with fresh colors and bold floral designs are adapted to the consumer and interior-design markets. The famed Spanish needlepoint industry, which outshone the knotted rugs in the early twentieth century, has now been largely taken over by Portugal.

In France, until the crusades, only flat-woven tapestries were made, notably in Tours and Arras. At this time, Saracenic rugs reached France and initiated a taste for novel floor and furniture coverings. However, it was not until the reign of Henry IV in the late sixteenth century that the Savonnerie workshop was established, producing at first copies of Oriental designs using the Turkish knot. (The Savonnerie was named after a soap factory, the former occupant of the premises.) Then Pierre Dupont, a former illuminator, obtained license from the king to head the Savonnerie industry. He proceeded to study

EUROPEAN RUGS

SPAIN

FRANCE

Plate 83
SHUSHA KARABAGH, 14' x 7'
wool, c. 1900
This area made rugs for the Russian and European market
combining rose sprays with native borders.

167

the art of Turkish rug-making, publishing his results in a pompous dissertation. During the seventeenth century, the Savonnerie workshop produced original rugs of excellent quality for use by the royal family. The rugs came in a variety of patterns to suit the tastes of the age, favoring popular Baroque and Rococo motifs, as well as pastoral and historic scenes. A palace-size rug illustrates the architectural framing and paneling devices used, imitating gilt boiseries and brocades enriched with bouquets of flowers in full bloom (plate 84).

The Gobelins ateliers had a similar product and history as the Savonnerie workshops. The finest Gobelins weaving was done for the French court with cartoons inspired by the artist decorator, Charles Lebrun.

The Aubusson workshop, located in the Creuse Valley, rivaled the Savonnerie. The rugs followed the same historical trends as the Savonneries, and LeBrun and other famous painters were commissioned to provide designs. Production peaked under Louis XIV, then declined. In the 1920s, the French artist Jean Lurçat revived the Aubusson looms to accommodate the cartoons of Picasso, Matisse, and other great artists. Today, under the guidance of the French Ministry of the Arts, Aubusson continues to produce, often on a commission basis, high-quality workmanship carefully following the older methods. Requests for these rugs come from all over the world. At Gobelin, a school and a museum are attached to the current workshop which produces woven works of art comparable in quality to Aubussons.

ENGLAND

The earliest known interest in rug weaving in England began when Eleanor of Castile, Edward I's Spanish bride, brought a large selection of Moorish rugs to England in the thirteenth century. Edward III encouraged weaving in the fourteenth century by inviting Flemish craftsmen to settle in England. By the sixteenth century rugs became the focus of international intrigue and prestige. Cardinal Wolsey through political and economic pressure acquired over sixty from Venetian trade merchants. His famous lot of sixty Turkish carpets in 1520 was a sure sign of growing fascination with Oriental rugs.

By the seventeenth century, English royalty had established factories to rival the similar weaving centers set up in France and Spain. Domestic wool was plentiful, and workshops sprang up in Mortlake, Norwich, Wilton, and Axminster, the latter founded by Thomas Whitty in the eighteenth century. The

Plate 84
SAVONNERIE, 30' x 20'
wool, c. 1875
Formerly in the collection of King Farouk of Egypt.
An exact copy of this rug was made for the Hotel Carlyle
in Japan.

170

highly durable rugs produced in this period resemble French and Spanish work, with an admixture of Turkish elements. The Adams brothers from Scotland, famous as architects and interior designers, designed and commissioned rugs in a severe classical style to compliment their buildings. In the nineteenth century, mechanized processes entered the field of rug weaving with Richard Wytock's invention of chenille weave, which soon monopolized weaving. The machine-made rug industry boomed in several locations, especially in Scotland.

The aesthetic stagnation brought on by machine technology in the late nineteenth century spurred John Ruskin and William Morris to demand a return to the original sources of the ancient craft of weaving rugs. An emphasis on good dyes and quality craftsmanship characterized Morris's efforts to revive the art. Morris and other artists popularized the curving floral motifs of Art Nouveau that became the vogue in rugs designed around the turn of the century. At this time England made excellent rugs, needlepoint, and other textiles. Since World War I, however, virtually no major looms for handmade rugs have been active, probably because of the high cost of labor.

* * * * *

Although Germany, Austria, Poland, Italy, the Netherlands, and Scandinavia never manufactured rugs in any quantity, the wealthy of these countries always avidly collected and studied these woven works of art. Today, Germany ranks as one of the foremost buyers of Oriental rugs and has sponsored many major exhibitions of them.

Plate 85
HEREKE, 7'10" x 5'8"
silk on silk foundation, 20th Cent.
Silk rugs are still woven in Hereke with great artistry
and craftsmanship as seen in this example.
(Collection of Glen Kalil, Oriental Rug Imports, Miami)

CHAPTER XI

CURRENTLY AVAILABLE AND NEW RUGS

The Oriental rugs available on the current market fall into two general categories: rugs woven over twenty years ago, termed "old" rugs, and those produced with the last two decades, commonly called "new" rugs by the trade. Through usage, dispersal, and lower levels of production in the past, there are far fewer old rugs on the market today than new rugs. Many traditional old rug types are no longer being woven today and are in demand by virtue of their rarity. Still, one can find many beautiful new rugs that closely follow the old patterns, particularly in the great traditional weaving centers. Two distinct markets exist for each of these categories, with considerable variation in cost depending on the type of rug, its condition, and current tastes in decoration.

OLD RUGS

Old rugs, dating from the nineteenth and early twentieth centuries, have been dealt with in earlier chapters, so here we will treat only the types that have grown relatively scarce and which therefore represent greater investment potential for the collector.

Tribal Rugs

Old tribal rugs in general have become very rare because of the disappearance of the nomadic or semi-nomadic life-styles of the people who made them. The Ghasghai, Bakhtiari, Kurd, Lori, and Baluchi, for example, have fallen victim to the wave of modernization in Iran that attracted much of the tribal population to wage-earning opportunities in the cities.

The abandonment of small village workshops has also meant a decrease in production over the past few decades. The materials have deteriorated with the disappearance of the finest wool blends and the elaborate, often secret, traditional processes of natural dyeing. Many tribal or village weavers found employment with city workshops; their new rugs, however, belong to the bales of mass-produced items geared for the big department-store trade. In former times, working for domestic demand, they wove rugs to be used by their own families or villages for weddings, birthdays, and other festive occasions. The full range of the weaver's originality and individuality was called upon to make these rugs. Significantly, the weavers rarely used cartoons, but altered memorized designs to suit the mood of the occasion. In contrast, the lifeless, monoto-

Plate 86
QUM, 7'2" x 4'7"
silk with silk foundation, c. 1960
Ghum has beacome famous for its production of high quality
silk rugs. This piece has a traditional garden design.

nous factory rugs, for which workers are paid by the square foot, reflect the lack of inspiration caused by pre-set patterns, synthetic dyes, and mediocre wool.

Some city workshops (a very select few) maintained high reputations into the early twentieth century for their standards of excellence. Examples of these are the Mohtasham of Kashan, the Hadji Jalili of Tabriz, and the Amoghli of Mashad (plates 12, 2, 10). However, these workshops could remain economically feasible only as long as the cost of high quality labor and materials was a small fraction of that in industrial countries. Today, even if we assembled the most gifted weavers, the time involved in raising the appropriate sheep for the wool and in preparing the suitable vegetable dyes would elevate the cost to astronomical levels.

City Workshops

European rugs were always in short supply on the market, since Aubussons and Savonneries, for instance, were made to order and in small quantities. Often the rugs remained with the family who commissioned them, or went to museums. In the early twentieth century, these elegant sophisticated rugs were the last word in completing an interior decorated with French period furniture. A recent change in fashion trends has brought a somewhat lessened demand for the rugs, so that these well-made and decorative pieces are a wise investment at today's prices.

European Rugs

Other types of old rugs have also grown scarce because of fashion trends. Serapi and Heriz rugs, for example, are among the most sought-after of traditional Persian types because of their suitability to the American decorative market and their compatibility with contemporary furniture styles. The ensuing shortage has raised prices considerably for these types of rugs.

Scarcity

Yet other kinds of rugs are scarce because of the lower durability of their materials, or because of the smallness of the original output. Fewer silk rugs have been made, for instance, than wool rugs, due to the high cost of quality silk and the great amount of time and skill required to knot this fine material. In addition, silk rugs perish more easily as they are subject to the effects of climate.

In contrast to the foregoing, recently made rugs appear on the market in abundance from a variety of sources and in a great range of quality. Of

NEW RUGS

Plate 87
TABRIZ, 6'8" x 4'9"
wool, c. 1970
A high quality modern rug with a very fine weave and a
traditional Hadji Jalili design.

course, the politics and economics of the rug-producing countries affect the availability of rugs. Recent developments in Iran and Afghanistan caused many refugees to flee these countries, bringing their assets with them in the form of rugs, thus temporarily flooding the market.

Iran

Until the late 1960s, Iran led the way in producing new rugs. Factories with very high standards for materials and workmanship grew under royal patronage. In the 1970s, however, India, Pakistan, China and, more recently, Romania, began to take their share of the international market with a supply of inexpensive pieces designed for Western tastes. Iran, however, commands respect for the continuance of its long tradition of master weavers, quality materials, tightness of weave, and coherent design. In terms of quality, Iran still ranks highest among producers of new rugs.

Weaving centers in Tabriz, Qum, Nain, Isfahan, and Kashan, all have large workshops and modern equipment. Each center, of course, produces rugs varying in quality and price. Some of the better known trade names for long-term investment include Serafian, Amir-Chatri, and Nejand. Isfahan, Qum, and Nain take the lead with the highest-quality silk rugs, with knot counts as high as 600–800 per square inch. A cautionary note: like Bordeaux wine, not all rugs tagged Tabriz or other famous names were made in the town itself; they may have been made in neighboring regions.

The recent modernization and consequent turmoil in Iran has undoubtedly affected rug production. With oil playing an ever-increasing role in Iran's economy, many weavers abandoned their looms, producing a labor shortage in the weaving industry. Social legislation provided raises for weavers, leading to a relatively high cost of labor compared to other rug-producing countries; the result being, since 1974, a shortage of rugs and an approximate doubling of prices. The recent revolution leads one to speculate that the greater compensation for weavers and the shortage of merchandise will combine to produce a further increase in prices. However, this upward trend may be counteracted in time by larger numbers of Iranians returning to traditional ways, including weaving. For the present, we should remember that importers have large stocks on hand, in addition to the many pieces arriving with Iranian immigrants who cannot take money out of the country. This means that the market has yet to feel an actual shortage.

Plate 88
KERMAN, 8'2" x 5'2"
wool, c. 1960
A Bird of Paradise meditation rug from a center that continues to produce high quality pieces.

Pakistan has emerged as a major producer of decorative rugs and a competitor with Iran and India in terms of quantity, with the majority of rugs being shipped to the United States and West Germany. Since the creation of this country in 1947, Pakistan has benefited from the immigration of large numbers of skilled weavers from the Indian cities of Amritsar and Mirzapur to Lahore and Karachi. In the 1960s, private capital financed new workshops and greatly improved the quality of production.

Pakistani weavers mostly imitate traditional Persian and Turkoman patterns, heavily doctored to please the Western eye. In Pakistan and India, private commissions have notably increased for rugs tailored to the needs of Western clients. The favorite designs are Kerman, Sarouk, Bokhara, Kafkazi (Caucasian), Tekke, Saryk (called "Sarooki" in the trade), and Yomud without the traditional dark red colors. A wool called "mori" gives these rugs a particularly soft and lustrous appearance. Marked improvement in the quality of dyes (as a result of surveillance by dye masters, known as "ustads") has decreased reliance on chemical washes.

India has now surpassed Iran in its production of new rugs, using techniques, patterns (variations of older Persian, Turkish, and Chinese designs), and a sales philosophy similar to that of Pakistan. In May 1978, according to *Rug News,* India's output was double that of Iran's. In many cases, the government actively helped this production by training weavers. Unfortunately for many years, loose weaving and poor wool often resulted in rough-pile rugs with a tendency to shed, but recently the quality shows remarkable signs of improvement. Kashmir silk rugs tend to be one of the better grades. Obeetees is one of the leading companies in rug production. Inexpensive Pakistani dhurries in cheerful colors have lately become a popular item with decorators and can be found in convenient sizes in Western department stores.

Afghanistan saw a great promotion of its rug-export industry in the late 1940s, which brought changes to the cottage industry largely composed of women. The new workshops instituted since the mid-1960s have male weavers, as women rarely work outside the home. Traditional designs continue to be woven, featuring the Mari (Saryk and Tekke) patterns, Ersaris

Pakistan

India

Afghanistan

Plate 89
TEHRAN, 7'2" x 4'9"
wool, early 20th Cent.
This is a meditation rug with a design named after a
famous woman weaver Hadji Khanomi.

179

with tight weaves, Baluchis, and Golden Afghans (so called because of the new yellow introduced in 1929). More recently, patterns combining Persian and Turkish designs have been successfully introduced. The rugs still come in small sizes, usually woven on wool, sometimes cotton, warp and weft, with golds and corals slowly replacing the reds of old. Fairly good examples of hatchli rugs (some very fine ones in silk) can be found at relatively high prices, although they are still less expensive than the Persians.

Turkey

Turkey, in the face of the competition, has been taking steps to recover her former preeminence in rug weaving. In 1952, the Sumer National Bank, the official bank of Turkey, supported a revitalization of the industry and traditional master-weavers were sought to institute training programs. Today, women still perform most of the weaving, but many work for village cooperatives as well as in the traditional home cottage industry. Since the 1970s, private entrepreneurs have entered the field and brought new standards of quality; however, the quality does not equal that of the older generations of Greeks and Armenians, and production still lags behind India, Iran, Pakistan, and China. Although the labor costs less than in some other countries, the materials cost more, making the overall cost of rug production similar to other competing countries. With the tremendous rise in the cost of living, workshop owners hoard the finest pieces as hedges against inflation, which effectively keeps them off the market.

Most of the rugs produced derive from older styles, and the prayer-rug format, such as Melas-Ghiordes, remains the most popular design. Government-operated plants at Hereke, Bursa, Kirshehir, Konya, Kayseri, Sivas, and Imrali turn out some of the finest pieces (plate 85). Superb silk rugs, especially Herekes and Bursas, have tight weaves and a rich, subtle palette of pastel colors. Less fine pieces usually consist of sturdy wool, thick pile, and cotton foundations. Many of the rugs receive a wash similar to that of the new "antique finish" Chinese rugs. Turkey also produces a large number of kilims in geometric designs, with a tendency towards garish coloring.

China

At the end of World War II, China took advantage of the reorganization following the revolution to dramatically modernize and step up rug production. For several years, the heavy Western tariffs on Chinese imports made

Plate 90
BERGAMA, 6′5″ x 4′5″
wool, c. 1950
A new rug from this old Turkish rug center.

commerce almost prohibitive; however, recent legislation has lowered the tariffs and should result in a major increase in Chinese imports.

In the early 1970s the Chinese began to favor a process called "antique" finish, whereby a chemical wash produces a rich luster similar to older rugs. Chinese rugs closely follow traditional designs, but have a thicker pile than older pieces. Cutting off the pile to achieve a sculptured effect endangers the foundation of the knots and decreases the durability of the piece, making this practice a technical weakness in Chinese rugs. Inexpensive labor and recent quality control should make for relatively affordable, decorative rugs. Nevertheless, the rugs, including those from the chief centers at Tientsin, Ninghsia, Peking, and Tsinanfu, lack originality. Recently, the Chinese have begun to make silk rugs, imitating Persian designs and very similar to those coming out of Pakistan. China now accepts more private commissions for rugs.

Greece and Bulgaria are considerably below China in production levels, though they received a fair share of excellent weavers in the 1920s, following the exodus of Greeks and Armenians from Turkey. Rug production of moderate quality in these two countries continues in small, privately owned and regulated workshops. **Greece Bulgaria**

In contrast to Greece and Bulgaria, Soviet Union workshops are heavily controlled by the State. They continue to produce Caucasian rugs in various modern versions, usually lacking the inspiration of former times. Armenia and Azerbaijan, still the major areas of rug weaving, employ standardized old designs, using both natural and chrome dyes. In the Baku area, Turkish weavers make rugs with bright colors and favor the old Kazak, Karabagh, and so-called Kabistan designs. Occasionally, pictorial rugs may be found; these most often have an ideological content, perhaps a portrait of Lenin or the cosmonauts. A heavy export duty makes rugs from the Soviet Union non-competitive on today's market. **Soviet Union**

Romania also has State-operated rug factories. A move in recent years to expand the country's rug industry has had notable results. Again, the community of Armenian weavers originating from Turkey played a key role. The Arta Populari cooperative of Bucharest provides the best source of well- **Romania**

Plate 91
AFSHAR, 13'1" x 6'2"
wool, c. 1875
A very rare and fine rug with a Moharemati design.

184

185

made copies of traditional, appropriately knotted, Persian or Turkish design rugs woven in a high-quality mix of New Zealand, Australian, and domestic yarns. These decorative rugs are increasingly popular with designers.

Hungary

Hungary has followed in Romania's footsteps in its attempt to modernize rug production. Its output consists of folkloric thick wool rugs and kilims, often incorporating natural colors, as well as silk rugs, few of which have yet reached the international market.

Portugal

Portugal has always echoed Spanish production. Currently, they make needlepoint work in the style of Aubussons, mostly on commission.

New rugs represent an investment inasmuch as they are an investment in lifestyle. They can set an image of sophistication and elegance at an affordable price, especially in comparison with machine-made carpeting. Well-made new rugs will outlast wall-to-wall floor coverings. They also have considerable resale value, whereas the machine-made carpeting has virtually none. In 1980, the Oriental Rugs Importers Association in New York stated that a good quality 12-by-9 foot modern Tabriz, sold in 1975 for $2,500, would now sell for $9,000. A Heriz has risen over the same period from $1,500 to $5,000, a Kashan has gone from $2,000 to $9,000. In other words, an increase of almost 300 percent has been realized in some cases.

Those collectors who hope to find better prices in the wholesale market will find that prices are rapidly reaching those of the retail market. With the great abundance of available new rugs, it cannot be emphasized too often that, as with dealing in old rugs, one must establish a good relationship with a reputable dealer.

Plate 92
FERAHAN, 6' x 4'3"
wool, c. 1900
A very beautiful piece with a Moharemati design and
a characteristic green in the border.
(Private Collection, New York)

186

MAJOR EXHIBITIONS

Allen Art Museum Rug Exhibition, Oberlin, Ohio.
Ancient Art of the Asian Steppes and Highlands. Los Angeles County Museum of Art, from July 25, 1978.
Antique Chinese Carpets: Masterpieces from the David Te Chun Wang Collection. Rippon Boswell, London, 1978.
Kaukasische Teppiche. Kunst und Gewerbe, Hamburg, 1961; Frankfurt, 1962.
Old Caucasian Rugs. Damianich Janos Muzeum, Szdnok, April 1–May 28, 1978; Iparmüvészeh Múzeum (Museum of Applied Arts), Budapest, June 28–October 30, 1978.
Rugs in Private Collections (Teppiche in Privatsammlungen). Mutmassungen über eine Knüpfenn.
Spanish Rugs in Madrid (Exposicion de alfambras antiquas espàñoles), 1933.
Stars of Spain. Textile Museum, Washington, D.C., March 31–July 1, 1978.
Ten Great Carpets. Boston Museum of Fine Arts, Autumn 1977.
The Adil Besim Exhibition of Oriental Carpets. Kursalon, Stadpark, Vienna.
Turkoman Rugs from the Ashkhabad Museum in Paris. Musée de l'Homme, Trocadero, Paris, Summer 1979.

MUSEUMS AND MAJOR COLLECTIONS

Beirut, Nicolas Sursock Museum
Berlin, Islamic Department, Berlin Museum
Berlin, Kunstgewerbe Museum
Boston, Museum of Fine Arts
Cairo, Museum of Islamic Art
Chicago, Art Institute
Cleveland, Cleveland Museum of Art
Cologne, Kunstgewerbe Museum
Cologne, Schurmann Collection
Florence, Bardini Museum
Hamburg, Kunst und Gewerbe Museum
Istanbul, Türk ve Islam Eserleri Museum
Jaipur Museum
Konya, Mevlana Museum
Leningrad, Hermitage Museum

London, Victoria and Albert Museum
Los Angeles, County Museum of Art
Lyons, Musée Historique des Tissus
Milan, Poldi Pezzoli Museum
Munich, Bavarian National Museum
New York, Metropolitan Museum of Art
Paris, Gobelins Museums
Paris, Louvre; Musée des Arts Décoratifs
Philadelphia, Museum of Art; Williams Collection
Qum, Shrine of the Mosque
Rothschild Collections
Stockholm, National Museum
Tehran, National Museum
Vienna, Angewandte Kunst Museum; Hapsburg Collection
Washington, National Gallery; Textile Museum

Plate 93
DAGHESTAN PRAYER, 4'9" x 3'8"
wool, c. 1850
An early example with a tightly controlled design and
color scheme from an area which produced many prayer rugs.

188

189

BIBLIOGRAPHY

BOOKS

Benardout, R. *Caucasian Rugs.* Raymond Benardout, England, 1978.

Böde, W. *Vorderasiatische Knüpteppiche.* Verlag von Hermann Seemann Nachfolger, Leipzig, n.d.

--- *Altorientalishe Tierleppiche.* Vienna, 1892.

Bogoliouboff, A.A. *Tapisseries de l' Asie Central.* St. Petersburg, 1908.

Breck, J. and Morris, F. *The Ballard Collection of Oriental Rugs.* New York, 1923.

de Calatchi, R. *Oriental Carpets.* Charles E. Tuttle Company, Rutland, Vermont, 1967.

Clark, H. *Bokhara, Turkoman, and Afghan Rugs.* John Lane and Bodley Head Ltd., London, 1922.

Coen, L. and Duncan, L. *The Oriental Rug.* Harper and Row, New York, 1978.

Dilley, A.U. *Oriental Rugs and Carpets.* Revised edition, M.S. Dimand, Lippincott, New York, 1959.

Erdmann, K. *700 Years of Oriental Carpets.* Berkeley, University of California Press, 1970.

--- *Oriental Carpets—An Essay on their History.* New York, 1962.

Edwards, A.C. *The Persian Carpet.* Duckworth, London, 1953.

Eiland, M. *Oriental Rugs.* New York Graphic Society, Boston, 1976.

Emery, I. *The Primary Structure of Fabrics.* The Textile Museum, Washington, D.C., 1966.

Fogg Catalogue, foreword by Joseph V. McMullan; introduction and notes by Christopher Dunham Reed. Cambridge, Massachusetts, Harvard University, William Hayes Fogg Art Museum, 1966.

Franses, J. *European and Oriental Rugs for Pleasure and Investment.* Arco, New York, 1970.

Gans-Ruedin, E. *Antique Oriental Carpets.* Kodansha International, Tokyo, 1975.

--- *The Connoisseur's Guide to Oriental Carpets.* Charles E. Tuttle, Rutland, Vermont, 1971.

Hackmack, A. *Chinese Carpets and Rugs.* Translated by L. Arnold, Tientsin-Peking, La Librairie Française Tientsin, Peiyang Press, 1924.

Hawley, W. *Oriental Rugs.* Dodd, Mead, and Co., New York, 1922.

--- *Oriental Rugs, Antique and Modern.* Dover Publications, New York, 1970.

Holt, R. B. *Rugs, Oriental and Occidental.* Garden City Publishing Company, Garden City, New York, 1937.

Hubel, R. G. *The Book of Carpets.* Praeger, New York, 1970.

Iten-Maritz, J. *Turkish Carpets.* Kodansha International, Tokyo, 1977.

Izmidlian, G. *Oriental Rugs and Carpets Today.* Hippocrene Books, New York, 1977.

Jacobsen, C. *Check Points on How to Buy Oriental Rugs.* Charles E. Tuttle, Rutland, Vermont, 1967.

Kendrick, A. F. and Tattersall. *Hand-Woven Carpets:Oriental and European.* New York, 1973.

Kerimov, L. *Azerbaijan Carpets.* Baku, 1961.

Landreau, A. and Pickering, W. *From the Bosporous to Samarkand, Flat-Woven Rugs.* The Textile Museum, Washington, D.C., 1969.

Lewis, G. *Practical Book of Oriental Rugs.* Lippincott, Philadelphia, 1911.

Lorentz, H. A. *A View of Chinese Rugs from the Seventeeth to the Twentieth Century.* Routledge and Kegan Paul, London, 1973.

Mazzini, F. *Tappeti Orientali.* Leghorn, 1950.

McMullan, J. and Reichert, D. *The George Walter Vincent and Belle Townsley Smith Collection of Islamic Rugs.* George Walter Vincent Smith Art Museum, Massachusetts, n.d.

Mumford, J. K. *Oriental Rugs.* Scribners, New York, 1900.

O'Bannon, G. *The Turkoman Carpet.* Gerald Duckworth and Co., London, 1974.

Pakzad, M. *Persische Knüpfkunst.* Kleeblatt Verlag fr. Grimsehl Hannover, 1978.

Pope, A. U. *A Survey of Persian Art.* London, 1938-39.

Raphaelian, H. *Rugs of Armenia.* An Anatol Sivas Publication, New York, 1960.

Reed, S. *Oriental Rugs and Carpets.* Putnam, New York, 1967.

Plate 94
KUBA (BAKU), 5′5″ x 3′4″
wool, c. 1840-50
A very fine early example with a dense complex design
of leaf brackets and stepped polygons.

BIBLIOGRAPHY

Schurmann, V. *Caucasian Rugs*. The Crosby Press, Wheathold Green, Ramsdell, Basingstoke, England, 1974.

Schürmann, U. *Central Asian Rugs*. Verlag Osterneth, Frankfurt, 1969.

--- *Oriental Carpets*. Paul Hamlyn, London, 1966.

Thacher, A. B. *Turkoman Rugs*. E. Weyne, New York, 1940.

The Academy of Arts, Istanbul. *Eski Türk Halilarindan ve Kilimlennden Örnekler*. Sümer-bank, Turkey, 1961.

The Tiffany Studios. *Antique Chinese Rugs*. Charles E. Tuttle Company, Rutland, Vermont, 1970.

Tschebull, R. *Kazak*. Introduction by Joseph V. McMullan, Near Eastern Art Research Center, New York Rug Society, 1971.

Turkoman Rugs. Foreword by Joseph V. McMullan; introduction and notes by Christopher Dunham Reed. Harvard University, William Hayes Fogg Art Museum, Cambridge, Massachusetts, 1966.

Victoria and Albert Museum Guide to the Collections of Carpets, London, 1931.

Weeks, J. and Treganowan, D. *Rugs and Carpets of Europe and the Western World*. Weathervane Books, New York, 1969.

Welch, S. *A King's Book of Kings*. New York Graphic Society, Connecticut, 1972.

ARTICLES

"A guide to collecting Oriental art." *Business Week*, August 20, 1976, pp.122–126.

"Are Oriental rugs a hedge against inflation." *The Designer*, April, 1978, pp.56–58.

"Before you invest in an Oriental rug." *Business Week*, January 23, 1978, pp.101–102.

Blau, D. "What you should know about Oriental rugs." *Trusts and Estates*, August, 1979, pp.23–27.

DeWitt, K. "How Iran unrest affects rug trade." *New York Times*, February 15, 1979.

Ettore, B. "Bonanzas from the bazaar: Oriental rugs." *New York Times*, August 12, 1979 (see Investing).

Hutt, J. "Uncovering the perplexities of Oriental rug racket." *Antiques Monthly*, August, 1979.

McQuade, W. "Flying high on magic carpets." *Fortune*, May, 1968, p.162.

Nemati, P. "Rugs as an investment." *Antiques and Art*, Fall 1979, pp.50–53.

"Oriental rug dealer." *The Wall Street Journal*, 1973.

Reif, R. "Rugs:Some Prices Are Still Climbing" *The New York Times*, April 1980

Rush, R. H. "Antique Rugs as an Investment." *The Wall Street Transcript*, 1974.

--- and the editors of U.S. News and World Report Books. "Investments you can live with and enjoy." *U.S. News and World Report*, 1974.

Ryder,W. "Carpet price rises loom." *Middle East Economic Digest*, Vol.23, no.28, July 13, 1979.

"The High Flying Carpet." *Investment Alert* newsletter, June 1979, pp.3–6.

Plate 95
SHIRVAN, 5′ x 3′3″
wool, early 20th Cent.
A typical design with a rare yellow field.

GLOSSARY AND SHORT INDEX

Abdul Mejid. Turkish ruler from 1839 to 1861 who established royal looms at Hereke in 1844. (See p.59, *111*)

Abrash. The varying intensities of a given color on a rug, usually visible on the field of older tribal rugs. It is caused by several factors: the different susceptibility of the strands of yarn to dye; the length of time yarn is left in the dye vat; the exposure of the dyed wool to the sun; and the use of different dye lots. It usually indicates age and is now prized by connoisseurs. (See p.71)

Adams Brothers. Robert (1728-1792), James (1730-1794) British architects and furniture designers.

Afghan Gul. Turkoman lozenge-shaped medallion. (See p.147)

Afshar. Southeast Persian tribal rug-weaving center. (See p.58, *106*, plate 36)

Agra. Northwest Indian rug-weaving center. The *Agra design* is a repeat pattern composed of a flowering plant enclosed in a rectilinear medallion. (See p.86, 151, plate 75)

Akbar. Indian Mogul emperor from 1556 to 1605 and art patron. (See p.62)

Ala-ad-din Mosque. Noted mosque in Konya, Turkey, originally built by the Seljuks and housing some of the earliest surviving Seljuk rug fragments. (p.58)

Alcaraz. Sixteenth- and seventeenth-century Spanish weaving center. (p.167)

Allahabad. North-central Indian rug-weaving center on the Ganges. (p.154)

Alpujarra. Spanish weaving district. (p.167)

Altai Mountains. Major Asian mountain range in U.S.S.R., Mongolia and China. (p.63)

Altman, B. American rug collector and importer. (p.22)

American Auctioneer's Association. (p.22)

Amir-Chatri. Trade name for fine Persian rugs. (p.178, plate 22)

Amoghli Mashad. Fine workshop in Mashad, in northeastern Persia. (p.*103*, 175 plate 10)

Amritsar. North Indian rug-weaving center. (p.154)

Anatolia. Plateau of western Turkey, a region noted for rug weaving. (p.58, *107*)

Angora. Southeastern Turkish weaving center near the Persian border. *Angora wool* is a high-quality goat wool. (p.70, *115*)

Aniline. Chemical dyes, invented by a Swiss chemist, began to be manufactured in the 1860s. (p.71, 75)

Antique finish. Chemical treatment of new rugs to give the appearance of age. (p.183)

Arabesque design. Ornate floral and foliate vine motif often appearing on Persian rugs. (e.g., p.110, plate 24)

Arabic dating and numbers. (p.67)

Arak. Weaving district in the North Western area of central Persia. (p.99)

Ardebil Carpet. Rug originally in the Ardebil Mosque, now in the Victoria and Albert Museum, dated 1529-1540. (p.*18, 19*, 34, 35) *Ardebil design* refers to central octagon-shaped grid with arabesque and scroll motifs. (e.g., p.98, 102, plate 2)

Armenians. Ethnic group located primarily around the Black Sea and in Turkey, the Caucasus, and Eastern Europe, noted for their weaving. (p.63, *126)*

Arta Populari. Modern Romanian rug-weaving government cooperatives. (p.183)

Ashik. Turkoman Yomud motif in the form of a lozenge. (p.147)

Asymmetrical knot. See knot. (p.78)

Aubusson. French weaving atelier. (p.66, *170, 175*)

Auctions. (p.51)

Avars. Nomadic tribal people. (p. 63)

Axminster. English weaving center active from 1756 on. (p.66, 170)

Azerbaijan. Mountainous region in the Caucasus. (p.91, 98, 106, 134, 183)

Azo Dyes. Twentieth century chemical dyes. (p.75)

Babur. Mogul ruler from 1526 to 1530 and art patron who encouraged rug weaving in India. (p.59, 151)

Bafande. Persian word for weavers. (See foreword)

Bakshaish. Rug-weaving center in an area near Ferahan in north central Persia. (p.98)

Baktiari. Rug district in central Persia. (p.102, 174, plate 37)

Baku. Rug district in the southern Caucasus. (p.122, 126, 134, 183)

Baluchi. Turkoman tribe near the eastern border of Persia noted for rug weaving. (p.106, 150, 174, 182, plate 72, 73)

Bangalor. East Indian weaving center. (p.154)

Benguiat, Vitall. International rug dealer (1860-1934). (p.22)

Plate 96
PEREPEDIL (KUBA), 4'11" x 3'7"
wool, late 19th Cent.
A rug similar to Plate 20, this example has a chalice
and leaf border.

Berberyan, Stephan. Noted American nineteenth-century rug dealer. (p.23)

Bergama. Western Anatolian rug-weaving center. (p.59, 62, 111, 115, plates 54, 90)

Beshire. Turkoman rugs made by a subgroup of the Ersari tribe. (p.147, plate 71)

Bidjar. Northern central Persian rug weaving district. (p.42, 99, plate 30)

Bidjov. Caucasian Field pattern design. (p.134)

Bordjalou-Kazak. Northern Caucasian rug district in Kazak tribal area. (p.126, 127, plate 60)

Bokhara. City in northeast Turkestan, after which a broad variety of rugs are commonly named. (p.139, 147, plate 71) (Princess Bokhara p.67)

Boteh (Mir). An ancient tear-shaped floral motif composed of flowering bushes which inspired the paisley design. (See paisley motif, p.106, 115, e.g., plate 102)

Bursa. Turkish weaving center in Western Anatolia noted for silk rugs. (p.59, 107, 182)

Cabbage Rose. European floral motif adapted by Caucasian weavers. (p. 134, e.g., plates 83, 84)

Cartouche. Oval or oblong design which encapsulates an inscription. (e.g., p.19, e.g., plate 2)

Cecim (cicim, djidjim). Flat-woven rug technique with slit construction. (p.118)

Chelaberd-Kazak. Central Caucasian weaving center in the Kazak district. (p.127, 130, See Eagle Kazak, plate 17)

Chichi. Caucasian weaving center in the Baku district. (p.135, plate 18, drawing p.123) *Chichi border.* Caucasian border of alternating diagonal bars and rosettes. (See drawing)

Chi'en Lung. Chinese emperor from 1736 to 1796, patron of the arts. (p.62, 158)

Chinchilla. Fifteenth-century Spanish weaving center. (p.66, 167)

Chodor. Turkoman rugs made by a subgroup of the Yomud tribe. (p.147)

Chondzoresk. Northern Caucasian weaving center in the Kazak district. (p.130)

Chrome dyes. Chemical dyes which were developed in the 1940s. (p.75)

Chub-bash. Turkoman rugs made by a subgroup of the Ersari tribe. (p.147)

Cintamini. Royal Turkish design consisting of two wavy lines crowned by three dots, thought to have originated in the 17th century. (p.59)

Cochineal. Bluish-red insect-based dye. (p.74)

Comb. Caucasian and Turkish pronged motif often appearing on prayer rugs. (p.123, e.g., plate 137)

Costikyan. American import-export firm founded in the late 19th century. (p.22, 94)

Crab border. Caucasian and Turkish floral pattern similar in shape to a crab. (plate 99)

Dabir. Trade name for fine kashans. (p.102)

Daghestan. Southern Caucasian weaving center in the Shirvan district noted for its prayer rugs. (p.126, 135, plate 93)

Deering, Charles. Noted nineteenth-century American rug collector. (p.23)

Derbend. Rugs from the eastern Caucasus on the Caspian Sea. (p.63, 126, 135)

Dhurrie. Flat-woven rugs frequently made in India and Pakistan. (p.39, 179, plate 32)

Dole, Andrew Rollins. Noted nineteenth-century American rug collector. (p.26)

Dragon. Chinese motif symbolizing good fortune and royalty. (p.66, 163, e.g., plate 78)

Dragon Carpets. The oldest surviving Caucasian rugs, depicting stylized dragons. (p.119)

Dupont, P. Major cartoonist and weaving master at 16th century Savonnerie workshops. (p.167)

Dyes. Color agents (natural, aniline, azos, chrome). (p.74-75)

Eagle Kazak. Rugs from southwestern Caucasus, dominated by two or three large diamond-shaped medallions adorned with Maltese Crosses (sunburst motif). (p.50, 127, plate 17)

Eight Emblems. Chinese Buddhist symbol. (p.166)

Eight Precious Things. Chinese symbols from the "one hundred symbols" of the Book of Rites.(p.163)

Eight Trigrams. Chinese I-Ching symbols. (p.163)

Ersari. Turkoman tribe that wove rugs in the Manguishlak district. (p.147, 179, drawing p.147, plate 21) *Ersari Gul.* (See drawing)

Fatpur. Royal 16th-century rug-weaving center in northwest India. (p.62, 151)

Ferahan. North-central Persian rug-weaving center. (p.99) *Ferahan Sarouk* is the finest grade of Sarouk rug, from north-central Persia. (p.86, plates 44, 92)

Fields, Marshall. Noted American rug collector and major importer at the turn of the century. (p.(100) p.22)

Flat-weaves. See kilim, cecim, dhurrie. (p.115-118, 135, plate 32)

Fu. Chinese character for bat, symbol of good luck. (p.163)

Fu Dog (Shitzu). Chinese mythological animal, a cross between a dog and a lion. (p.163)

Plate 97
SHIRVAN, 4'9" x 3'11"
wool, early 20th Cent.
The medallions in the field design derive from
the Lesghi tribe.

197

Garden design. Persian floral motif popularized in 16th century, thought to represent paradise. (p.91, e.g., plates 42, 86)

Gendje. Rugs from the northeast Karabagh area of the Caucasus. (p.66, 122, 123, 127)

Ghasghai. Tribal rugs from southwest Persia. (p.58, 106, 174, plates 49, 101)

Ghastili. Persian import-export firm based in Kerman, Iran. (p.94)

Ghiordes. Rugs from the Turkish Anatolia region, notably prayer rugs. (p.59, 182, plates 6, 50)

Gobelin. French tapestry and rug atelier founded in 1607. (p.170)

Gorovan. Northwest Persian rug-weaving center in the Heriz district. (p.98)

Gul (Guli). Octagonal decorative motif frequently appearing on Turkoman rugs. (p.91)

Gul Hinani (Gel henai). Persian motif figuring the henna flower. (drawing)

Hadji Jalili. Noted Tabriz weaver. (p.98, 175, plate 5, 11)

Hadow, C. M. English exporter of Indian rugs, c.1900. (p.154)

Hamadan. Northwest Persian rug district noted for runners. (p.70, 99, plate 35)

Hankow. Eastern Chinese weaving center on Yangtze Kiang. (p.155)

Haroon. South-central Persian weaving center. (p.102)

Hatchli (Engsi). Turkoman design seen on door hangings. (p.143, plate 68)

Herat, Herati. Northeast Persian weaving center. (p.00) *Herat pattern* is an abstract Persian floral design with a diamond-shaped rosette flanked by four leaves, often used to cover the whole field. (p.58, 91, e.g., plate 00, drawing)

Hereke. Turkish royal looms founded by Abdul Mejid in 1844; also Turkish rugs noted for their silks. (p.39, 59, 86, 110, plates 9, 52, 85)

Heriz. Northwest Persian rugs from a district near Tabriz. (p.98, plates 1, 3, 45)

Holbein. Type of design found on rugs in paintings by Hans Holbein the Younger (1497-1543). These rugs carry a kufic border and octagonal medallions interlaced with knots. Rugs with similar designs originated in Turkey. (p.66)

I-Ching. "The Classic of Changes." Ancient Chinese book used to predict the future by employing hexagrams or six-line patterns. (p.163)

Imreli. Anatolian weaving center active in the production of new Turkish rugs. (p.182)

Indigo. Natural dye from the indigo plant, producing many shades of blue. (p.74)

Isfahan. Southern Persian weaving center. (p39, 86, 102, 178, plate 8)

Joshaghan. Central Persian weaving center. *Joshaghan design*, a diamond-shaped grid inscribed with large geometric rosettes and arabesques.

Jufti Knot. (p.79)

Juval. Turkoman bag often used as a cushion. (p.142)

Kabistan. Legendary rug center of the Caucasus; often a misnomer for Shirvans. (p.138)

K'ang Hsi. Chinese emperor from 1662 to 1722, patron of the arts. (p.62)

Karabagh. Northwest Persian rug-weaving center. (p.66, 119, 123, 127, 130, 183, plates 66, 83)

Karachov-Kazak. Northeast Caucasian rugs. (p.126, 127)

Kashan. South-central Persian weaving center noted for fine quality rugs and for silks. (p.39, 58, 86, 102, 178, 186, plates 12, 13, 47)

Kashgar. Semi-nomadic East Turkestan weavers. (p.155)

Kashmir. Indian weaving center. (p.103, 151, 179)

Kayseri. Central Turkish weaving center, noted for silks. (p.85, 182)

Kazak. Tribal weaving district in the northwest Caucasus. (p.62, 86, 122, 123, 183, plates 17, 56, 57, 58, 59, 60, 99)

Kazvin. Misnomer for a northwest Persian type of Hamadan, properly known as Hamadan-Shahrbaff. (p.95)

Kerman. Rugs from southeast Persia. *Kerman Laver*, a type of Kerman rug. (p.58, 74, 94, 103, plates 88, 102)

Kervorkian, Hagop. Noted early twentieth-century American collector. (p.23)

Kilim. Flat-weave technique with no pile. Kilims are thin and reversible. (p.39, 78, 106, 135, 182, 186, plates 30, 31)

Kirshehir. Central Turkish rugs. (p.115, 182)

Kiz Ghiordes. Double prayer niche motif found on Turkish Ghiordes prayer rugs, usually symbolizing matrimony. (p.111)

Khila. Southern Caucasian weaving center in the Kuba district. (p.126, plate 62)

Khorassan. Northeast Persian weaving district. (p.55, 102)

Konya. Central Turkish weaving center, noted for prayer rugs. (p.59, 114, 182)

Kork. Extremely fine Persian wool similar to Manchester wool. (p.70)

Plate 98
SEICHUR, 6'5" x 4'
wool, early 20th Cent.
This piece contains the "running dog" border with a
Bidjov type field design.

Kuba. Rugs from the eastern Caucasus. (p.66, 122, 131, 134, plates 20, 66, 94, 100)

Kufic. Ancient Arabic calligraphy script popularized in the 6th century. *Kufic border* chain device based on kufic script. (p.134)

Kula. Turkish weaving center in central Anatolia, noted for prayer rugs. (p.111, 114, plate 24)

Kurdistan. Western Persian weaving district. (p.126, 174)

Ladik. Central Turkish weaving center, noted for prayer rugs. (p.59, 114)

Lahore. Royal rug-weaving center in northwest India. (p.62, 151, 179)

Latchhook. Decorative S-shaped motif usually adorning medallions and borders in Caucasian and Turkoman rugs. (p.123)

Laver Kerman. Type of Kerman rug produced in the neighboring town of Raver. (p.103, plate 46)

Lenkoran. Caucasian weaving center on the Caspian Sea, specializing in runners. (p.126, 130, plate 63)

Lesghi. Northwestern Caucasian weaving center. (p.63, 122, 134, 135)

Leturi. Spanish weaving center. (p.167)

Looms. Upright, rolltop, nomadic. (p.79, 123)

Lotto. Design found on rugs in paintings by the Venetian painter Lorenzo Lotto (1480-1556), consisting of a repeated pattern of serrated, interlocking geometric leaf forms and arabesques. (p.18, 110) Star Oushak (p.110)

Lotus. Chinese floral pattern. (p.166)

Madder. Vegetable dye producing many shades of red, used throughout the East. (p.74)

Mahajeran. Fine grade of Sarouk from north-central Persia. (See also Ferahan Sarouk) (p.99)

Mahal. Type of Sarouk from north-central Persia. (p.75, plate 74)

Makri. Turkish weaving center in southern Anatolia. (p.114)

Malayer. Northwest Persian weaving center. (p.95)

Mameluke carpets. Rugs made under Egyptian and Turkish rulers from the 14th to the 16th centuries, usually manufactured in Cairo or Damascus. (p.59, plate 26)

Mar (Merv) Gul. Turkoman Salor tribal device. (p.142, drawing p.142)

Marasali. Caucasian weaving center in the Shirvan district, noted for prayer rugs. (p.126, 131, plate 67)

Mari. Afghanistan trade name for Saryk and Tekke rug patterns. (p.179)

Marquand, H. Noted turn-of-the-century American rug collector. (p.22)

Mashad. Northwest Persian weaving center in the Khorosan district. (p.102, 103, plate 10)

McMullan, Joseph V. Noted American turn-of-the-century rug collector. (p.23)

Melas. Turkish weaving center in southwest Anatolia, noted for prayer rugs. (p.59, 114, 182, plate 25)

Mercerized cotton. Cotton given a silky sheen through a process invented by the Englishman John Mercer (1791-1866). Also known as polished cotton. (p.71)

Meshkin. Northwest Persian weaving center. (p.98)

Mihrab. Prayer niche appearing in mosques and on prayer rugs which indicates the direction of Mecca for prayer. (p.110, e.g., plate 71)

Mina Khani. An overall floral motif possibly originating in Kurdistan, composed of guls (flowers) arranged in a diamond pattern. (p.91)

Ming dynasty. Chinese rulers from 1368 to 1649. (p.00) *Ming rug fragment.* Chinese carpet fragment in the collection of the Metropolitan Museum of Art. (p.158)

Moghan. Southeastern Caucasian weaving center. (p.126, 131)

Mohtasham Kashan. Noted workshop in Kashan in north-central Persia. (p.175, plates 12, 13)

Mordant. Substance that fixes the dye color. (p.71)

Morris, William. Nineteenth-century English artist and designer. (p.171)

Mortlake. English weaving center founded in the eighteenth century. (p.66)

Mudejar. Turkish weaving center in central Anatolia. (p.115, 167)

Nain. New rugs from the Isfahan district in southeast Persia. (p.102, 178)

Natanz. Central Persian weaving center. (p.102)

Ninghsia. Weaving district in north-central China; also generic name for high-quality Chinese rugs. (p.155, 183)

Norwich. English weaving center. (p.66, 170)

Obeetees. Indian rug trade name. (p.179)

O'Donnovan, Edward. Traveler among Turkoman tribes, c. 1880. (p.142)

Osmolduk. Turkoman five-sided rug. (p.143)

Plate 99
GENDJE KAZAK, 6′11″ x 4′11″
wool, early 20th Cent.
A rare type of Kazak with a distinctive "crab flower"
border. This piece is in mint condition.

Oriental Carpet Manufacturers. English exporters of Indian rugs, c. 1900. (p.00)

Oushak. Ancient Turkish rug-weaving center in central Anatolia. (p.59, 86, 110, plate 53)

Pashmina. Goat hair of the highest quality from Himalayan mountain goats. (p.103)

Pazyryk Carpet. Oldest preserved rug fragment, discovered in 1949 in the Altai Mountains, dating from 500-300B.C., possibly of Turkic origin. (p.35, 55)

Peking. Chinese weaving center on the northern Chinese sea coast; also generic name for Chinese rugs. (p.39, 62, 183, plate 76)

Perepedil. Eastern Caucasian rug-weaving center, featuring a distinctive design of stylized rams' horns; also known as *Wurma*. (p.126, plate 96)

Persian knot. See knots. (p.78, 126)

Petag. Noted 19th-century exporter of Persian rugs based in Tabriz. (p.98)

Phoenix (feng-huang). Chinese and Persian mythological bird thought to be reborn every thousand years. (p.71, e.g., plate 77)

Pile. Yarn forming the surface of a rug. (p.75, 78)

Prayer rug. Rug used for praying in Islam. (p.110, plates 67, 68)

Qualin. A Turkoman rug larger than 9′ x 6′. (p.143) **Qualincha.** A Turkoman rug smaller than 9′ x 6′.

Qum (Ghum). Recent rug-weaving center in central Iran noted for fine rugs and silks. (p.86, 102, 178, plate 86)

Robinson, Vincent. The London dealer who purchased the Ardebil Carpet in 1888. (p.18, 19)

Roller-beam loom. Upright loom with two moveable beams. (p.00)

Rudenko S. I. Soviet archaeologist whose team discovered the Pazyryk Carpet (see Pazyryk). (p.55)

Safavid. Persian dynasty from 1501 to 1736. (p.35, 55, 59, 91, 94)

Saffron. Extremely valuable golden-yellow vegetable dye. (p.102)

Salor. Rugs from the Salor Turkoman tribe located around the Merv River. (p.139, 142, 146)

Sarouk. Persian rug weaving center (p.38, 75, 86, 94, 99, plates 14, 38, 48)

Saryk Gul. Turkoman motif of the Saryk tribe located north of Afghanistan. (p.139, 142, 146, 179)

Savonnerie. French rug atelier founded in 1628. (p.114, 175, plate 84)

Seichur. Eastern Caucasian rug-weaving center near the Caspian Sea. (p.126, 135, plates 64, 82, 98)

Seljuk. Turkish dynasty ruling over central and western Asia from the 11th to the 19th century. (p.58, 59, 63, 107)

Selvedge. Border reinforcement sewn along the sides of a rug.

Senneh (Sehna). See knots. (p.178, drawing p.78) Senneh, Northwest Persian rug weaving center (p.75, plate 33)

Serafian. Trade name for high-quality modern Persian rugs. (p.102, 178)

Serab. Persian weaving center (p.70)

Serapi. Northwest Persian weaving center in the Heriz district. (p.35, 39, 42, 86, 98, 175, plates 4, 15, 27, 42)

Sewan-Kazak. Caucasian Kazak rug design. (p.126, 127, plate 57)

Shah-Nemah. Book recounting famous Persian legends. (p.35, 102)

Shah Tahmasp. Persian ruler from 1524 to 1576. (p.55)

Shantung. Chinese rug-weaving district along the China Sea. (p.62)

Shawls. (p.103)

Shiraz. Persian rug center in southern Iran. (p.106)

Shirazi. Flat-woven border binding the ends of certain tribal rugs, has a similar function to a kilim skirt border.

Shirvan. Southeastern Caucasian rug district noted for prayer rugs. (p.86, 122, 126, 131, 134, plates 16, 19, 28, 29, 61, 95, 97)

Shou. Round Chinese motif. (p.163)

Sileh. Flat-weave technique thought to have originated in the Caucasus. (p.78, 135)

Sileh Kazak. Northern Caucasian rug with dragon motif. (p.127, plate 58)

Silk Route. Major commercial caravan route for the silk trade from China to Turkey via the Caucasus. (p.63)

Sivas. Southeastern Turkish weaving center near the Persian border. (p.115, 182, plate 51)

Slitweave. Flatweave technique. (p.78)

Sloane, W. J. Noted turn-of-the-century American rug collector and importer. (p.22)

Srinagar. Rugs from northern India. (p.154)

Suleiman the Magnificent. Ottoman ruler from 1520 to 1566. (p.107)

Sultanabad. See Arak. Central Persian rugs. (p.99)

Soumak (sumac, sumak, sumakh). Flat-weave technique. (p.78, 135, plates 33, 34)

Plate 100
KUBA, 6′9″ x 4′4″
wool, c. 1880
A Kazak type "crab flower" border and a rare white field
distinguish this piece.

Surahani. Rugs from the Azerbaijan district of the Caucasus. (p.134)

Swastika. Ancient Chinese Z-shaped motif. (p.158, 162)

Tabriz. Weaving center in northwest Persia. (p.35, 39, 58, 94, 98) *Tabriz loom.* An upright loom with adjustable warps. (p.79, 115, 178, 186, plates 2, 5, 11, 22, 87)

Talish. Eastern Caucasian rug-weaving center, specializing in runners. (p.126, 130, 131, plate 65)

Tarantula. Caucasian spider design used to avert the evil eye. (e.g., plate 00)

Taoism. Chinese philosophy which influenced rug decoration. (p.162, 166)

Tehran. Modern Persian weaving center. (plate 89)

Tekke. Turkoman tribal rugs from the area of Mashad in Iran. (p.142, 179, plate 69)

Tientsin. Chinese weaving center near Peking, in northern China close to the China Sea. (p.183)

Tree of Life. Ancient design of a tree symbolizing continuous and bountiful growth, appearing throughout the East. (p.103, e.g., plate 25)

Tsinanfu. Weaving center in central eastern China on the Hwang-ho river. (p.183)

Unicorn (Chi'lin). Chinese mythological beast, a horse with a long horn. (p.163)

Vase. Persian and Turkish rug design featuring a central medallion in the form of a vase holding flowers, thought to symbolize cleanliness and spirituality in Islamic tradition. (e.g., plate 89)

Verneh (Verne). Flat-weave technique. (p.78, 135)

Wanamaker, John. Noted American turn-of-the-century rug collector and importer. (p.22)

Wilton. English 18th-and 19th-century weaving center. (p.66, 170)

Yarkand. Eastern Turkestan weaving center. (p.158, plate 81)

Yerkes, Charles. Noted turn-of-the-century American collector. (p.23)

Yomud. Turkoman tribe along the banks of the Oxus River and eastern shores of the Caspian Sea. (p.146, plate 70) *Yomud Dyrnak Gul.* Turkoman octagonal medallion. (p.146, drawings p.143) *Yomud Ertmen Gul.* Turkoman octagonal medallion. *Yomud Kepse Gul.* Turkoman octagonal medallion.

Yoruk. Turkish weaving center (p.107, plate 55)

Ziegler Brothers. Manchester, England firm which sold the Ardebil carpet to Vincent Robinson. (p.19, 98)

Plate 101
GHASHGAI SADDLEBAG, 2' x 4'
wool with flatweave back, early 20th Cent.
This is a very fine example of a woven saddlebag by this
Persian nomadic tribe.

Several years ago, when this book was begun, I decided to travel across the United States in order to get to know the many dealers who share my enthusiasm for oriental rugs. This is a vast, wonderful country. The more time I spent travelling the more aware I became of the great number of interesting people in my profession. Just as I had intended to illustrate many more examples of oriental rugs and had, in the end, to limit the number of these plates so too I had to cut short my visits all over America.

The role of the dealer is a crucial one in investing in oriental rugs. During the preparation of this edition I have been privileged to meet and to speak with many fine dealers. I regret all those others whom time prevented me from seeing. It is my hope, for the second edition of *RUGS AS AN INVESTMENT* to have the opportunity to personally visit many other dealers.

The following listing of dealers is broken down by region and by special service. I suggest, to the readers of this book, that they build a long lasting relationship with the dealer of their choice. In the final analysis, it must be for the individual to select a dealer whose expertise he can respect and readily draw upon.

Alabama	Asia Rug Company, Inc. 408 Hollywood Boulevard, Birmingham, Ala. 35209. (205) 879-8244. Antique, Semi-Ant., New Rugs, All Types; Retail. Dir.: Jimile S. Shunnarah, Est. 1967. Rest., Clean., Appraisals, Lect.
	King's House Orientals 2418 Montevallo Road, Birmingham, Ala. 35223. (205) 871-5787. Antique, Semi-Ant., New Rugs, All Types; Retail/Wholesale. Dir.: Alice Schleusner, Est. 1972. Appraisals, Lect.
California	Iloulian Rugs 418 North La Cienega Boulevard, Los Angeles, Cal. 90048. (213) 659-2999. Antique, Semi-Ant., All Types, esp. Persian, Chinese, Caucasian; Retail/Wholesale. Dir.: M. Iloulian, Est. 1970. Rest., Clean., Appraisals
	Joseph and John Kilejian 8789 Beverly Boulevard, Los Angeles, Cal. 90048. (213) 657-3005/10. Antique, Semi-Ant., All Types esp. Nomadic, European, Period; Retail/Wholesale. Dir.: Joseph and John Kilejian, Est. 1973. Rest., Appraisals
	Pashaie Oriental Rugs Gallery 755 N. LaCienega Blvd., Los Angeles, Cal. 90069 (213) 657-0259/0250. Antique, Semi-Ant., New Rugs, All Types esp. rare & expensive; Retail. Est. 1969. Rest., Clean.,
	Rugs, Inc. 121 Pacific Design Center, 8687 Melrose Avenue, Los Angeles, Cal. 90069. Antique, Semi-Ant., New Rugs, All Types; Retail/Wholesale. Dir.: V. Deirmendjian, Est. 1969. Rest., Clean., Appraisals
	Kashian Persian Rugs 1610 El Camino Real, Menlo Park, Cal. 94025. (415) 327-0735. Antique, Semi-Ant., New Rugs, All Types esp. Ant. Caucasian; Retail/Wholesale. Dir.: Puzant H. Kashian, Est. 1908. Rest., Clean., Appraisals
	Rezaian Persian Rug Company 256 Shoreline Highway, Mill Valley, Cal. 94941. (415) 383-5733. Antique, Semi-Ant., New Rugs, All Types esp. Ant. Persian, Chinese; Retail/Wholesale. Dir.: Taghi Rezaian, Est. 1969. Rest., Clean., Appraisals
	Adil Besim & Company 370 Lake Avenue, Pasadena, Cal. 91101. (213) 795-7589. Antique, Semi-Ant., New Rugs, All Types; Retail/Wholesale. Dir.: Fritz Langauer, Ferdi Besim, Jack Hatounian, Est. 1946. Rest., Clean., Appraisals, Storage
	Agajeenian Oriental Rugs 4520 El Cajon Boulevard, San Diego, Cal. 92105. (714) 563-0922/23. Antique, Semi-Ant., New Rugs, All Types; Retail/Wholesale. Dir.: Robert Agajeenian. Est. 1966. Rest., Clean., Appraisals, Lect.
	Parse Rug Company 1100 Sutter, San Francisco, Cal. 94109. (415) 673-2777. Antique, Semi-Ant., All Types; Retail/Wholesale. Dir.: Amed Abraham, Rest., Clean., Appraisals
	Woven Treasures 816-A 4th Street, San Rafael, Cal. 94901. (415) 456-2111. Antique, Semi-Ant., New Rugs, All Types; Retail/Wholesale. Dir.: Isaac Moattar, Est. 1961. Rest., Clean., Appraisals
Colorado	Oriental Rug Gallery Limited 3342 East Colfax Avenue, Denver Col. 80206. (303) 355-0201. Antique, Semi-Ant., New Rugs, All Types esp. Tribal and Caucasian; Retail/Wholesale. Dir.: Martin Wirth, Est. 1942. Rest.
	H. Medill Sarkisian 693 East Speer Boulevard, Denver, Col. 80203. (303) 733-2623. Antique, Semi-Ant., New Rugs, All Types esp. Chinese; Retail. Dir.: H. Medill Sarkisian, Est. 1893. Rest., Clean., Appraisals
Connecticut	Tree of Life Gallery, Inc. 28 East Main Street, Old Avon Village, Avon, Conn. 06001. (203) 678-0234, 263-4830. Antique, Semi-Ant., New Rugs, All Types esp. Navajo, Persian; Retail/Wholesale. Dir.: Armand J. Dupré, Jr., Est. 1971. Rest., Clean., Appraisals
	Pasha's Rugs & Imports 337 North Main Street (Bishop's Corner), West Hartford, Conn. 06117. (203) 233-8188, 233-1619. Antique, Semi-Ant., New Rugs, All Types esp. Rare Period; Retail. Dir.: Mr. Pashaie, Est. 1969. Rest., Clean., Appraisals
	The Rugs of Persia 73 Elm Street, New Canaan, Conn. 06840. (203) 972-1944. Antique, Semi-Ant., New Rugs, Persian Only; Retail/Wholesale. Dir.: Mohammad Pashazadeh, Rosanne Maroufkhani, Est. 1977. Rest., Clean., Appraisals
	M.H. Kebabian 73 Elm Street, New Haven, Conn. 06510. (203) 865-0567. Antique, Semi-Ant., New Rugs, All Types esp. Persian; Retail. Dir.: M.H. Kebabian, Est. 1883. Rest., Clean., Appraisals, Lect.

Plate 102
KIRMAN SHAWL, 5'6" x 5'3"
pashmina wool, twill tapestry technique, c. 1800
Shawls were a mark of rank among the Eastern nobility and were in great demand in Europe throughout the 18th and 19th Century. These and other textiles will be the subject of an upcoming book.

Mussallem Oriental Rugs, Inc.   1922 Phoenix Avenue, Jacksonville, Fla. 32206. (904) 356-7177. Antique, Semi-Ant., New Rugs, All Types; Retail. Dir.: Charles Mussallem, Est. 1912 [Founders of Rug Retailers of America (1970)]. Rest., Clean., Lect.
Oriental Rug Imports   2000 Biscayne Boulevard, Miami, Fla. 33137. (305) 576-1771. Antique, Semi-Ant., New Rugs, All Types; Retail/Wholesale. Dir.: Glen Kalil.
Jinishian Oriental Rugs   863 North Orange Avenue, Orlando, Fla. 32801 (305) 423-2068. Antique, Semi-Ant., New Rugs, All Types; Retail. Dir.: Mr. Gabbayan, Est. 1940. Rest., Appraisals, Lect.
The Shah Abbas Collection   4307 El Prado Boulevard, Tampa, Fla. (813) 837-9800. [Branches: 1662 Main Street, Sarasota, Fla.; 245 Fifth Avenue, New York, N.Y. 10016. (212) 689-3444.] Antique, Semi-Ant., New Rugs, All Types esp. Late 19th C., 20th C. Persian; Retail (Fla.), Retail/Wholesale (N.Y.). Dir.: Jafar Falasiri, Est. 1979. Rest., Clean., Appraisals

Florida

Y. Albert & Son, Inc.   2303 Peachtree Road, N.E., Atlanta, Ga. 30309. (404) 355-0944. Antique, Semi-Ant., New Rugs, Retail/Wholesale. Dir.: Edward Y. Albert, Est. 1925. Appraisals

Georgia

Joseph W. Fell, Ltd.   3221 North Clark Street, Chicago, Ill. 60657. (312) 549-6076. Antique, Semi-Ant., All Types esp. Tribal; Retail. Dir.: Joseph W. Fell, Est. 1970. Rest., Clean., Appraisals, Lect.
Minasian Oriental Rug Company, Inc.   1244 Chicago Avenue, Evanston, Ill. 60202. (312) 491-0985. Antique, Semi-Ant., New Rugs, All Types esp. Persian; Retail/Wholesale. Dir.: Mr. Armen Minasian, Mr. Carnig, Est. 1897. Rest., Clean., Appraisals, Lect.
H.C. Nahigian and Sons, Inc.   5140 Gold Road, Skokie, Ill. 60077. (312) 676-2500. Antique, Semi-Ant., New Rugs, All Types. Dir.: Jack H. Nahigian, Jack C. Nahigian, Dee C. Nahigian, Est. 1910. Rest., Clean., Appraisals
Vartan V. Pedian & Sons, Inc.   6535 North Lincoln Avenue, Lincolnwood, Ill. 60645. (312) 675-9111. Antique, Semi-Ant., New Rugs, All Types esp. North African and Custom; Retail/Wholesale. Dir.: Haig Pedian, Est. 1906. Rest., Clean., Appraisals

Illinois

Kerman Rug Company, Inc.   17 East Maryland Street, Indianapolis, Ind. 46204. (317) 635-3901. Antique, Semi-Ant., New Rugs, All Types; Retail/Wholesale. Dir.: R.J. Benjamin, Sr., Est. 1921. Rest., Clean., Appraisals, Lect.

Indiana

Foster's Oriental Rugs   4905 Old Brownsboro Road, Louisville, Ky. 40222. (502) 426-0080. Antique, Semi-Ant., New Rugs, All Types esp. Rare Tribal, Heriz, Tabriz, Sultanabad; Retail/Wholesale. Dir.: Steve and Anna Foster, Est. 1971. Rest., Clean., Appraisals, Lect., Storage

Kentucky

Stephen Croft   204 Chartres, New Orleans, La. 70130. (504) 528-9215. Antique, Semi-Ant., All Types esp. Collector Rugs; Retail/Wholesale. Dir.: Stephen Croft, Est. 1978. Rest., Clean., Appraisals, Lect.
Safi Kaskas   240 Chartres Street, New Orleans, La. 70130. (504) 522-3200. Antique, Semi-Ant., New Rugs, All Types; Retail/Wholesale. Dir.: Safi Kaskas, Est. 1973. Rest., Clean., Appraisals, Lect.

Louisiana

Michael's Rug Gallery, Inc.   415 East 33rd Street, Baltimore, Md. 21218. (301) 366-1515. Antique, Semi-Ant., New Rugs, All Types esp. Caucasian; Retail/Wholesale. Dir.: Fahed B. Michael, Est. 1950. Rest., Clean., Appraisals
K.G. Borhani, Inc.   14 West Allegheny, Towson, Md. 21204. (301) 821-8060. Antique, Semi-Ant., New Rugs, All Types esp. Persian; Retail/Wholesale. Dir.: K. Borhani, Est. 1973. Rest., Clean., Appraisals

Maryland

Fine Arts Rug Inc.   1475 Beacon Street, Brookline, Mass. 02146. (617) 731-3733. Antique, Semi-Ant., New Rugs; Retail/Wholesale. Dir.: T. Chatalbash, Est. 1930. Rest., Clean., Appraisals
Persepolis Oriental Rug, Inc.   358 Washington Street, Wellesley Hills, Mass. 02181. (617) 237-1770 Antique, Semi-Ant., New Rugs, All Types; Retail/Wholesale Dir.: Ali Sadeghpour. Rest., Clean.
G. Pilibosian Rugs   1237 Main Street, Concord, Mass. 01742. (617) 369-6872. Antique, Semi-Ant., New Rugs, All Types; Retail. Dir.: George Pilibosian, Est. 1966. Rest., Clean., Appraisals
Toros Omartian & Son, Inc.   286 Bridge Street, Springfield, Mass. 01103. (413) 736-1531. Antique, Semi-Ant., New Rugs, All Types; Retail/Wholesale. Dir.: Toros Nishan Omartian, Steven N. Omartian, Est. 1919. Rest., Clean., Appraisals, Storage
Charles Yenian Company, Inc.   57 Pearl Street, Springfield, Mass. 01105. (413) 737-0368. Antique, Semi-Ant., New Rugs, All Types; Retail/Wholesale. Dir.: Albert Yenian, Est. 1920. Rest., Clean., Appraisals
Koko Boodakian & Sons   1026 Main Street, Winchester, Mass. 01890. (617) 729-5566. Antique, Semi-Ant., New Rugs, All Types; Retail/Wholesale. Dir.: Levon Boodakian, Est. 1938. Rest., Clean., Appraisals, Lect., Storage

Massachusetts

Michigan   Nigosian Carpet Company   21919 Michigan Avenue, Dearborn, Mich. 48124. (313) 277-1331. Antique, Semi-Ant., New Rugs, All Types esp. Persian, Retail. Dir.: George Nigosian, Est. 1970. Rest., Clean., Appraisals
Hagopian and Sons, Inc.   1400 West Eight Mile Road, Oak Park, Mich. 48237. (313) 399-2323. Antique, Semi-Ant., New Rugs, All Types; Retail. Dir.: Edgar Hagopian, Est. 1938. Rest., Clean., Appraisals, Lect.

Minnesota   Var Keljik Oriental Rug and Antique Gallery   1089 Grand Avenue, St. Paul, Minn. 55105. (612) 222-1197. Antique, Semi-Ant., All Types esp. Tribal and Caucasian; Retail. Dir.: Var Keljik, Est. 1897

Missouri   Azad Inc.   410 Nichols Road, Kansas City, Mo. 64112. (816) 931-9425. Antique, Semi-Ant., New Rugs, All Types; Retail/Wholesale. Dir.: Mr. Azad, Est. 1976. Rest., Clean., Appraisals, Lect.
Asadorian Rug Company, Inc.   8466 Natural Bridge Road, St. Louis, Mo. 63121. (314) 382-6605. Antique, Semi-Ant., New Rugs, All Types esp. Persian; Retail/Wholesale. Dir.: Edward Z. Asadorian, Est. 1945. Rest., Clean., Appraisals, Lect.

Nevada   Grand Persian & House of Oriental Rugs   M.G.M. Grand Hotel, Las Vegas, Nev. 89109. (702) 736-1440. Antique, Semi-Ant., New Rugs, All Types, Retail/Wholesale. Dir.: Mr. Alexander, Est. 1960. Rest., Clean., Appraisals

New Jersey   Starr Oriental Rugs   One Grand Avenue, Englewood, N.J. 07631. (201) 569-9024. Antique, Semi-Ant., New Rugs, All Types; Retail/Wholesale. Dir.: J. Massachi, Est. 1968. Clean., Appraisals
P.T.K. Inc.   327 Millburn Avenue, Millburn, N.J. 07041. (201) 376-0730. Antique, Semi-Ant., New Rugs, All Types; Retail/Wholesale. Dir.: Kashi Brod, Est. 1976. Rest., Clean.

New York   Charles Markarian and Sons, Inc.   3807 Delaware Avenue, Kenmore (Buffalo), N.Y. 14217. (716) 873-8667. Antique, Semi-Ant., New Rugs, All Types esp. Iranian and Indian; Retail/Wholesale. Dir.: Michael Markarian, Charles Markarian, Est. 1921. Rest., Clean., Appraisals, Gallery Talks

Antique Buyers International, Inc. 790 Madison Ave., New York, N.Y. 10021. (212) 861-6700. Antique, Semi-Ant., All Types, esp. Caucasian, Persian, Chinese, European, Tapestries: Retail/Wholesale. Dir. Parviz Nemati, Est. 1965. Rest., Clean., Appraisal, Portfolio management

A. Beshar & Company, Inc.   49 East 53rd Street, New York, N.Y. 10022. (212) 758-1400. Antique, Semi-Ant., New Rugs, All Types; Retail. Dir.: Lee Howard Beshar, Est. 1898. Rest., Clean., Appraisals, Lect.
John C. Edelmann Galleries, Inc.   123 East 77th Street, New York, N.Y. 10021. (212) 628-1700. Antique, Semi-Ant., New Rugs, All Types; Auctions. Dir.: John C. Edelmann, Est. 1979. Appraisals
The Ghiordian Knot Ltd.   1050 Second Avenue — Gallery 55, New York, N.Y. 10022. (212) 722-1235. Antique, Semi-Ant., New Rugs esp. silk Hereke, Isphahan, All Types esp. Investment Pieces, Tribal; Retail/Wholesale. Dir.: Barbara Z. Sedlin, Est. 1972. Rest., Clean.
Marvin Kagan, Inc.   991 Madison Avenue, New York, N.Y. 10021. (212) 535-9000. Antique, Semi-Ant., All Types; Retail. Dir.: Marvin Kagan, Est. 1953. Rest., Appraisals, Lect.
M. Kazemi & Company, Inc.   827 Franklin Avenue, Garden City, N.Y. 11530. (516) 294-6520. Antique, Semi-Ant., New Rugs, All Types esp. Persian, Chinese, Indian; Retail/Wholesale. Dir.: M. Kazemi, Est. 1970. Rest., Clean., Appraisals
Mehdi Dilmaghani & Company, Inc.   540 Central Park Avenue, Scarsdale, N.Y. 10583. (914) 472-1700. Antique, Semi-Ant., New Rugs, All Types; Retail/Wholesale. Dir.: Dennis A. Dilmaghani, Est. 1928. Rest., Clean., Appraisals

North Carolina   Oglukian Oriental Rugs, Inc.   4600 Oglukian Road, Charlotte, N.C. 28211. (704) 366-1972. Antique, Semi-Ant., New Rugs, All Types; Retail. Dir.: Raymond Oglukian, Est. 1940. Clean., Appraisals

Oklahoma   John Y. Iskian, Importers   6430 North Western Avenue, Oklahoma City, Okla. 73116. (405) 848-5353. Antique, Semi-Ant., New Rugs, All Types; Retail. Dir.: John Iskian, Est. 1928. Rest., Appraisals, Lect.

Ohio   Richard R. Markarian, Inc.   101 West 4th Street, Cincinnati, Ohio 45202. (513) 621-4122. Antique, Semi-Ant., New Rugs, All Types; Retail. Dir.: Richard R. Markarian, Bill Glasgow, Est. 1936. Rest., Appraisals, Lect.
K.A. Menedian, Inc.   1090 West Fifth Avenue, Columbus, Ohio 43212. (614) 249-3345. Antique, Semi-Ant., New Rugs, All Types; Retail/Wholesale. Dir.: K.A. Menedian, Est. 1909. Rest., Clean., Appraisals

Oregon   James Opie Oriental Rugs, Inc.   214 S.W. Stark Street, Portland, Ore. 97204. (503) 226-0116. Antique, Semi-Ant., New Rugs, All Types esp. Gashgai, Turkoman, Tribal, Caucasian, Kashans and Sarouks; Retail/Wholesale. Dir.: James Opie, Est. 1970. Rest., Clean., Appraisals, Lect.

Maqam   2815 West Queen Lane, Philadelphia, Pa. 19129. (215) 438-7873. Antique, Semi-Ant., All Types esp. Tribal; Retail. Dir.: Dennis Dodds, Est. 1975. Rest., Appraisals, Lect., American Editor *Hali*

M.G. Maloumian and Sons   7700 Germantown Avenue, Philadelphia, Pa. 19118. (215) 242-8655. Antique, Semi-Ant., New Rugs, All Types; Retail/Wholesale. Dir.: Richard and Royden Maloumian, Est. 1930. Appraisals, Lect.

Shihadeh Carpets   116 Cricket Avenue, Ardmore, Pa. 19003. (215) 649-2000. Antique, Semi-Ant., New Rugs, All Types; Retail/Wholesale. Dir.: T. David Shihadeh, Est. 1935. Rest., Clean., Appraisals

Amy M. Eways   40 South 5th Street, Reading, Pa. 19602. (215) 372-3446. Antique, Semi-Ant., New Rugs, All Types esp. Aubussons and Savonneries, Kilims, Custom; Retail/Wholesale. Dir.: Amy Eways, Est. 1924. Rest., Clean., Appraisals

Jerrehian Brothers   261 East Lancaster Avenue, Wynnewood, Pa. 19096. (215) 896-8800. Antique, Semi-Ant., New Rugs, All Types esp. Oversize, Rare, Silk; Retail/Wholesale. Dir.: Aram K. Jerrehian, Jr., Est. 1904. Rest., Clean., Appraisals, Storage

Pennsylvania

Alans Oriental Rug Company   1613 Union Avenue, Memphis, Tenn. 38104. (901) 276-5476. Antique, Semi-Ant., New Rugs, All Types esp. Seraphis; Retail. Dir.: Joel Bernsen, Appraisals

S.V. Kish Oriental Rugs, Inc.   [d/b/a Goldsmith's Oriental Rugs], c/o Goldsmith's Oak Court, 4545 Poplar Avenue, Memphis, Tenn. 38143. (901) 766-2361, 761-0114. Antique, Semi-Ant., New Rugs, All Types; Retail. Dir.: S.V. Kish, Est. 1940. Rest., Appraisals

Tennessee

Feizy Import & Export Company   196 Turtle Creek Village, Dallas, Tex. 75219. (214) 521-4600, 651-0877. Antique, Semi-Ant., New Rugs, All Types; Retail/Wholesale. Dir.: John Feizy, Est. 1972. Rest., Clean., Appraisals

Khan's Oriental Rugs   5028 Westheimer Road, Houston, Tex. 77056. (713) 960-8200. Antique, Semi-Ant., New Rugs, All Types; Retail/Wholesale. Dir.: Mohammed Akram Khan, Est. 1955. Rest., Repair, Weaving

Ami Negbi Gallery   2012 South Post Oak Road, Houston, Tex. 77056. (713) 965-0922. Antique, Semi-Ant., All Types esp. Rare; Retail. Dir.: E. Negbi, Est. 1965. Rest., Clean.

Sahadi's Gallery   1800 South Post Oak [In Sak's Fifth Avenue], Houston, Tex. 77056. (713) 626-4200. Antique, Semi-Ant., New Rugs, All Types esp. Serapis, Oushaks, Caucasians; Retail/Wholesale. Dir.: Edna Hadad Sahadi, Est. 1973. Rest., Clean., Appraisals

Texas

Shaia Oriental Rugs   Merchant Square [P.O. Box 61], Williamsburg, Va. 23185. (804) 220-0400. Antique, Semi-Ant., New Rugs, All Types; Retail. Dir.: Frank Shaia, Est. 1972. Rest., Clean., Appraisals

Virginia

Hanna Ayoub Oriental Rugs   5211 Wisconsin Avenue N.W., Washington, D.C. 20015. (202) 363-9200. Antique, Semi-Ant., New Rugs, All Types; Retail/Wholesale. Dir.: Hanna Ayoub, Est. 1929. Rest., Clean., Appraisals, Storage

Nazarian Brothers, Inc.   2323 Wisconsin Avenue, Washington, D.C. 20007. (202) 333-7800. Antique, Semi-Ant., New Rugs, All Types; Retail. Dir.: Elsie Nazarian, Est. 1920. Rest., Clean., Appraisals, Storage

Mark Keshishian & Sons, Inc.   6930 Wisconsin Avenue, Chevy Chase, Md. 20015; [Also] 836 Rockville Pike, Rockville, Md. 20854. (301) 654-4044, 340-6666. Antique, Semi-Ant., New Rugs, All Types esp. Collectibles and Large Tribal; Retail/Wholesale. Dir.: Mark, James and Harold Keshishian, Est. 1931. Rest., Clean., Appraisals, Lectures

Parvizian Inc.   7034 Wisconsin Avenue, Bethesda, Md. 20015. (301) 654-8989. Antiques, Semi-Ant., New Rugs, All Types; Retail/Wholesale. Dir.: Manoucher Parvizian, Est. 1972. Rest., Clean., Appraisals

Washington, D.C.

Barsamian Oriental Rug Gallery   603 North Milwaukee Street, Milwaukee, Wisc. 53202. (414) 276-2656, 276-3545. Antique, Semi-Ant., New Rugs, All Types; Retail/Wholesale. Dir.: Herb and George Barsamian, Est. 1914. Rest., Clean., Appraisals

Gabriel Rug Company, Inc.   420 East Wells Street, Milwaukee, Wisc. 53202. (414) 276-2840. Antique, Semi-Ant., New Rugs, All Types; Retail/Wholesale. Dir.: Lee Gabriel, Est. 1924. Appraisals

Wisconsin